SYMBOLS
OF
EGYPT

HEIKE OWUSU

SYMBOLS
OF
EGYPT

Sterling Publishing Co., Inc.
New York

Library of Congress Cataloging-in-Publication Data Available

10 9 8 7 6 5 4 3 2 1

Published by Sterling Publishing Company, Inc.
387 Park Avenue South, New York, N.Y. 10016
First published in Germany under the title *Symbole Agyptens* in 1998 by Schirner Verlag,
Darmstat
© 1998 Schirner Verlag
English translation © 2000 by Sterling Publishing Company, Inc.
Distributed in Canada by Sterling Publishing
^{C}/o Canadian Manda Group, One Atlantic Avenue, Suite 105
Toronto, Ontario, Canada M6K 3E7
Distributed in Great Britain and Europe by Cassell PLC
Wellington House, 125 Strand, London WC2R 0BB, England
Distributed in Australia by Capricorn Link (Australia) Pty Ltd.
P.O. Box 6651, Baulkham Hills, Business Centre, NSW 2153, Australia
Printed and Manufactured in the United States of America
All rights reserved

Sterling ISBN 0-8069-3545-6

TABLE OF CONTENTS

FOREWORD

Ancient Egypt owed its high culture to the Nile. Through the cyclic flooding of the land, a pronounced belief in the otherworld developed, which took the natural cycle of birth, death, and rebirth as its model. Although today we have received most of our information about this culture from their graves, the ancient Egyptians were an exceptionally life-oriented people who sought to drive thoughts of old age and death away to a great extent. Instead, the concepts of life in the otherworld and of rebirth were placed in the foreground. In order to be able to understand the world view that the Egyptians had, we must view it from a magical and spiritual angle.

The thinking of these people was not logical and rational, but image-symbolic. The magical principle applied that all powerful and great things are portrayed in small, apparently invisible things — both above and below, macrocosmos and microcosmos. On this basis, for example, the scarab was a symbol of the rising sun, and the sky could be represented as a cow. Because large things are portrayed in small things, one could influence the important processes in the world of the gods and the otherworld through symbolic ceremonies and portrayals. An inherent power, a kind of being or soul, is attributed to the symbols.

The ancient Egyptian religion incorporated an incomprehensible number of gods and their many embodiments. Gods — like people — were assigned a variety of personality characteristics, so that one and the same god could be represented in a wide variety of embodiments, split personalities, as it were. With this knowledge, understanding the very busy world of the ancient Egyptian gods becomes easier.

In the mythology, earthly life was strictly separated from the realm of the life of the gods. The only connecting link between the worlds was in the figure of the pharaoh. In this sense, he was not worshiped as a god himself. However, he had the task of taking care of the harmony between the worlds of the gods and the people. It was, therefore, within the scope of his authority to supervise adherence to religious rituals or to perform them himself.

In this book, an attempt will be made to bring the ancient Egyptians' understanding of themselves nearer to modern people and to explain the symbolic connections of their world view in such a way that they can be transported into the modern world.

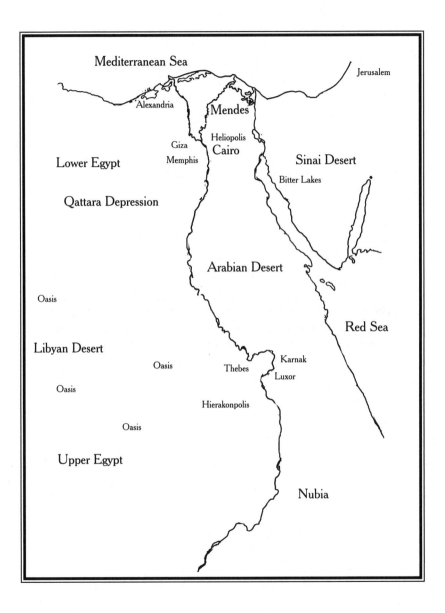

Time	Dynasties	Important rulers
Pre-Dynastic Era	1st Dynasty, 3100-2890	Scorpion, Narmer, Aha
Early Dynastic Era 3110-2181 BC	2nd Dynasty, 2890-2686	
to about 4000 BC		
Old Kingdom 2686-2181 BC	3rd Dynasty, 2686-2613	Zoser
	4th Dynasty, 2613-2494	Snofru, Cheops, Khephren, Mykerinos
	5th Dynasty, 2494-2345	Unas
	6th Dynasty, 2345-2181	
First Intermediate Era 2181-2040 BC	7th Dynasty, 2181-2173	
	8th Dynasty, 2173-2160	
	9th Dynasty, 2160-2130	
	10th Dynasty, 2130-2040	
Middle Kingdom 2133-1786 BC	11th Dynasty, 2133-1991	Sesostris I, Sesostris II, Sesostris III,
	12th Dynasty, 1991-1786	Amenemhat III
Second Intermediate Era 1786-1567 BC	13th Dynasty, 1786-1633	
	14th Dynasty, 1786-1603	
	15th Dynasty, 1674-1567	
	16th Dynasty, 1684-1567	
	17th Dynasty, 1650-1567	Rahotep
New Kingdom 1567-1085 BC	18th Dynasty, 1567-1320	Ahmose, Thutmosis I, Hatshepsut, Thutmosis II, Amenophis III (Teje), Amenophis III (Teje), Amenophis IV (Akhenaton/Nefertiti), Tutankhamen
	19th Dynasty, 1320-1200	Sety I, Ramses II, Merenptah, Siptah
	20th Dynasty, 1200-1085	Ramses III
Late Dynastic Era 1085-341 BC	21st Dynasty, 1085-945	
	22nd Dynasty, 950-730	
	23rd Dynasty, 817-730	
	24th Dynasty, 730-715	
	25th Dynasty, 751-656	
	26th Dynasty, 663-525	
	27th Dynasty, 525-404	
	28th Dynasty, 404-398	
	29th Dynasty, 398-378	
	30th Dynasty, 378-341	
Greek-Roman Era about 332 BC - 395 AD		Cleopatra

TIME TABLE

The division of the history of the country into three kingdoms and thirty dynasties goes back to a list prepared in the third century B.C. by Manetho, an Egyptian priest. Accordingly, a margin of error of 150 years is assumed, especially in the early dynasties.

If two or more dynasties in the table cover the same time, this means that they were recognized at the same time in different parts of Egypt.

SYMBOLS

The world view of the ancient Egyptians

THE EARTH AS A DISK

Like many peoples in this world, the ancient Egyptians also regarded their land as the navel of the world. Several politically influential cities, such as Thebes and Memphis, made a claim to have been built upon the original hill that once arose, in the beginning of time, from the original waters. The cradle of humanity lay at this place; it was therefore the starting point of all civilization. From this concept, the ancient Egyptians assumed the right to classify all other peoples as uncivilized and to consider the Nile land as a region favored by the gods.

The picture on the opposite page comes from the 4th millennium B.C.. On it, the Earth swims in the original ocean, which is represented by the outer ring. The Earth disk is carried by the ka sign in the lower center. The foreign peoples can be seen in the next largest ring, placed to the right and left of the gods of the East and the West. The winged sun rises above the entire motif. The next ring contains the symbols of the 41 regional standards. In the center, there is a stylized portrayal of the Nile land, with its gods, nobility, and working people.

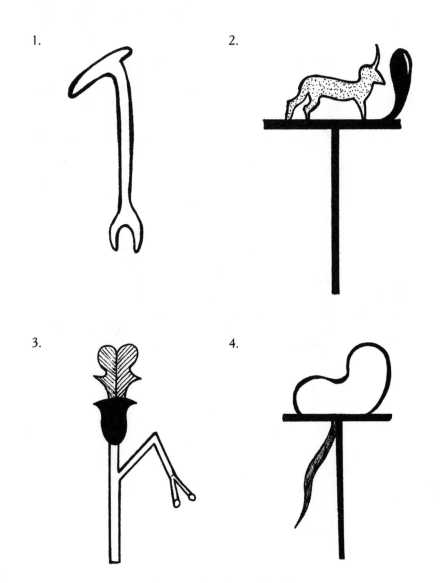

Scepters and standards

EMBLEMS OF THE GODS

1. The scepters represent a kind of amulet, with which a protective spirit in the shape of a fox or dog is associated. When placed in the hands of gods, they symbolize health and happiness. The uas scepter in Figure 1 consists of a forked staff with a dog's head at the upper end. It was placed in the grave with a dead person, in order to assure them the favor of the gods and a pleasant life on the other side. In many representations, two uas scepters bear the motif for heaven and in this way frame inscriptions. If the scepter is decorated with ribbons and feathers, this was the sign of the Thebes region and was called Uaset.

2. The staff amulet ukh played a role in the cult of Hathor and represents a pillar of heaven. This scepter, which consists of a papyrus stem and two feathers, was worshiped in Kusae.

Emblems that are attached to long rods were in use already in prehistoric times. They had great importance in processions and veneration of the king.

3. When a king died, he was accompanied to his grave by his god-standards. First came the standard of the Wepwawet, shown in Figure 3, which represents a dog, the divine path-opener. It was followed by a seated hawk, a standing ibis, the set animal, and the min sign, which consisted of a harpoon with two points.

4. The Khensu sign was carried at the end of the procession by the priest. The meaning of this sign has not been fully clarified. It shows either the placenta of the king, viewed as his twin and preserved in a container, or else the throne cushion.

In addition to the standards of the cult of the king, there were also regional signs and military standards.

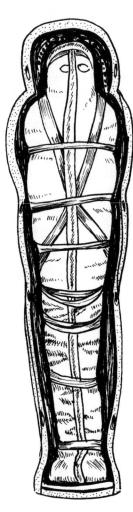

MUMMY

Since the Egyptians were convinced that body, spirit, and soul form an inseparable unit, they paid great attention to maintaining the physical body. According to their belief, the dead could initially live again only in their bodily form, and therefore preparation of the remains was undertaken with exceptional care. In spite of the expense involved, the mummy only characterizes a state of metamorphosis, the transformation of a living being into another form of existence within the eternally progressing cosmic spiral. In order to make this important step easier for the deceased person, his body was preserved as well as possible and subjected to a variety of rituals to guarantee life after death.

After the internal organs and the brain had been removed from the body, the body had to be dried for 70 days, a process that was supported by the hot climate and the salt content of the desert winds. The entrails were preserved in canopic jars, while only the heart was left in the body, since it played an important role before the court on the other side. The heart was weighed to see what kind of person the deceased was. After the drying, the mortal frame was filled with ground myrrh, casein, and fragrant herbs, sewn up, and then kept secluded for another 70 days. Then the remains were wrapped in linen strips and coated with rubber, after it had been cleaned again. The temple officials who had performed the embalming then gave the dead person to his relatives, who now decorated the body with a picture. According to the financial resources, the sarcophagus could be a life-sized, three-dimensional image of the deceased person that received the mummy or a painted portrait on a board or a sheet. Before the deceased person was transferred to the "House of the Eternity," the ritual of opening the mouth was performed, to make it again accessible to the life forces. After several sacrifice ceremonies to protect the deceased person on the other side, the sarcophagus was buried in the grave. On the great holidays, the relatives presented offerings at the graves for many years after the burial. People from the wealthy layers of society hired priests of the dead, already during their lifetimes, to hold a daily ceremony before their graves after their death.

This hieroglyphic in the form of a mummy stands both for the word itself and for the concepts connected with a transformation.

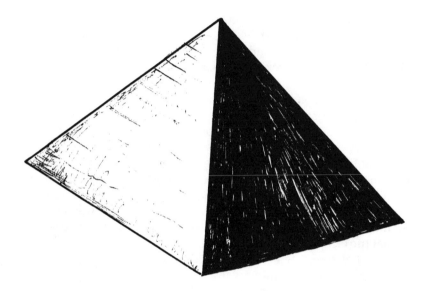

Pyramids — grave hills and energy stations

PYRAMID

The pyramids are surely the most striking monuments of the Old Egyptian culture, and they still present many riddles. Originally, they were to protect the grave, which was located in a space below the structure, from grave robbers. Their shape is often attributed to the old mastabas. In old times, the tip of the pyramid was covered with gold, in order to identify it as the seat of the sun god. Also, the structure is typically oriented toward the North Pole Star. Since the dead wanted to live there, an entrance pointed in this direction. The grave chamber was located in the west, the compass direction of the kingdom of the dead.

The largest of these structures, the pyramid of Cheops, also provides the greatest riddle. Often characterized as a book in stone, it was never used as a gravesite. It can be shown that its shape and orientation toward the north release a kind of energy, which provides maintenance of the life forces and aids to preservation. It is suspected that the great pyramids of Giza involve a kind of dedication center, in which the initiates are led through various stages to enlightenment. On the path, the disciple passes symbolically through the death process to the other side, then returns transformed to the world of the living.

It is fairly certain that the pyramid of Cheops was not built by the pharaoh of the same name, who, following an old tradition, only wanted to place his name in the structure. Lime deposits on the inside show that the pyramid must have stood under water, and they indicate a very early construction date, specifically about 10,000 B.C.. The many discoveries made in it have aroused such great interest that even today, an entire faculty of the University of Cairo is concerned exclusively with it.

Worn as an amulet, the power of the pyramid provides for mental fulfillment and vitalization.

1.

2.

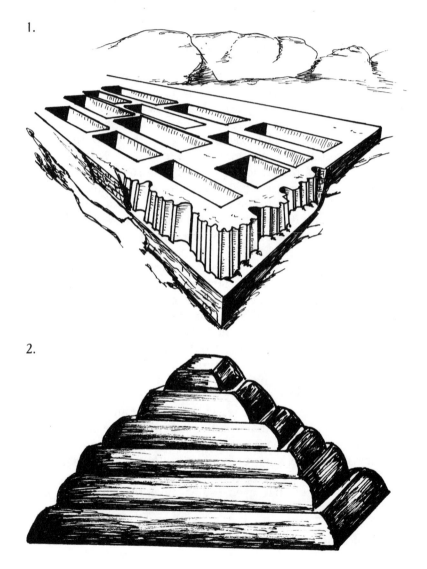

Early forms of pyramids

MASTABA

1. The mastabas involve an early form of the pyramid structures used later. The meaning of the word goes back to the Arabic word for "Bank" and relates to the rectangular shape of the structure. Originally, the Mastabas were built of clay bricks and wood elements. Their shape, which forms a flattened rectangle, symbolized the original hill that arose from the original waters and made life on earth possible. In these monumental tombs, the dead lay in a rectangular grave chamber in the middle of the structure. The symmetrically arranged supply chambers, which surrounded the underground grave, contained food, wine jugs, and objects of everyday life as gifts. These so-called "houses of eternity" also contained empty rooms as places for the dead to live in as well as bathtubs and toilets. Since the new spirit body of the dead needed no doors, no entrance of any kind was provided in such a system. A false door was included on the east side of the Mastaba, through which the deceased person could come out to receive offerings presented to him in his place of offering. This offering court was located between the surrounding wall and the main building. Structures of this kind were created already in the 1st Dynasty.

EARLY PYRAMIDS

2. These step pyramids were themselves often called mastabas. Their shape likewise represents a symbol of the original hill. The pyramid of Saqqara consists of six mastabas, one on top of another, which are smaller from bottom to top. Stone architecture of Egypt started in the Old Kingdom with this monument. The gigantic grave system of King Zoser extended underground and contained a large number of chambers for the dead.

Ornament with griffin

GRIFFIN

The drawing shows a portion of a piece of jewelry on which the pharaoh, in the form of a griffin, is trampling the enemies of Egypt. In the old times, the King was often represented as a lion with the head of a hawk. Like the hawk, the lion was also a solar symbol. The griffin was accordingly a blend of two fiery beings into an invincible mythological animal. Because of its invincibility rulers liked to have themselves portrayed in the pose of a victor as a griffin.

In the Middle Kingdom, the meaning of this symbolic animal changed into that of a protective demon who pulled the chariots of the hunters into battle against the beings of darkness; in Roman times, the gods Horus and Re took on the external form of the griffin.

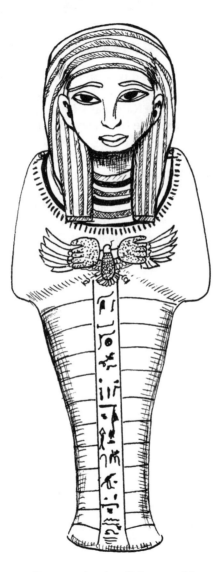

Servant in the Otherworld

SERVANTS

Mummy-shaped figures were given to the dead since the Middle Kingdom. As servants with magical gifts, they were to receive the expiatory work performed in the Other World. The Egyptians interpreted the name ushebti as "answerer," since whenever the deceased person was called to work, the ushebti would call "Here I am." In many graves, as many as 365 such figures have been found, one for each day of the year. In order for these images to be able to accomplish their work better, they often held tools in their hands, or in later times they were provided with painted tools. Also, some of them carried a bag of grains on their backs.

1.

2.

3.

Hieroglyphics for man, woman, and child

MAN, WOMAN, AND CHILD

1. In order to express a human being in general, he was represented in this resting pose. The hieroglyphic here stands for the word "man." Traditionally, the man is shown seated on a flat cushion, with his leg at an angle. The arms are likewise in a relaxed position. In order to convey the concept of maleness, the hands are shown clenched into fists.

2. The hieroglyphic for "woman," which describes the person herself, but also the female environment, shows a complete profile representation. Typical here are the wig and the robe, which covers the entire body and gives the sign the more of a hieroglyphic for "goddess." The sign embodies the ideal image of the Egyptian woman, the slender shape and a virtuous, reserved attitude. If women were portrayed in their traditional field, this related to their activities primarily in the areas of the home and motherhood.

3. This hieroglyphic shows a small child sticking his thumb in his mouth. It stands for the word "child." His posture shows that the child is sitting on his mother's lap. Egyptian women had an especially close relationship with small children, since they nursed them until the third year of life. Since milk was the most important means of prevention against diseases, children whose mothers had no milk or not enough were given to a wet-nurse.

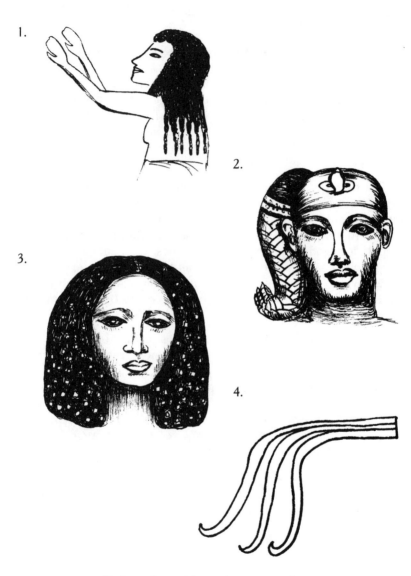

Hair styles with various meanings

HAIRSTYLES

Hairdos served in old Egypt to express personality, rank, or also certain emotional states of consciousness. Thus, for example, the disciples of the priesthood shaved their heads and bodies bald in order to demonstrate their subjection to the power of the gods. Women giving birth bound their hair into two firm bunches on top of the head in order to preserve their magical powers.

1. Open hair was general considered ugly and was tolerated in public, as shown in the drawing on the opposite page, only as a sign of mourning. Long, open hair was often seen on musicians and dancers as a means of erotic expression.

2. A sign of childhood was a lock growing out of the nearly bald-shaven head of a boy of the upper social levels. It also served as a symbol of eternal youth (see Khensu p. 69).

3. Higher officials and members of the court could be recognized by the use of wigs. In addition, the Egyptians associated a kind of erotic passion with this accessory. Women used artistic hair styles to strengthen their attractiveness to men. On certain social occasions, fragrant balls of ointment were worn on the head; they melted in the heat and let perfumed oil run over the shoulders. The drawing shows the head of a woman with cut hair and a removal wig decorated with golden pearls.

4. The hieroglyphic for "hair" consists of three locks together. They were also inserted into more complex words associated with sorrow or the character of a person.

31

1.

2.

Cosmetic utensils for the gods

MAKEUP PALETTE

The palette on the opposite page (inside and outside) from the pre-dynastic time shows a kind of early form of hieroglyphic writing. The slate plate probably served for grinding eye makeup for images of gods.

The four jumping dogs on the inside and outside embody the four celestial directions.

1. The palms framed by giraffes were meant to announce pleasant periods of peace, whereby giraffes were always viewed as symbolizing long vision and looking forward.

2. The inside of the object shows a depression for the paint, protected by powerful royal lions, by a mythical animal, and by the sacred ibis.

HEIROGLYPHICS

The ancient Egyptian picture writing represents a mixture of pictorial signs and written symbols that described a sound value. This combination made it especially difficult to decipher hieroglyphics. Other obstacles were the fact that some signs had several meanings and that some signs were connected with unusual associations.

The direction for reading hieroglyphic writing generally went from right to left. Since the signs only gave the sound value of the consonants and vowels were never written, the pronunciation of ancient Egyptian words can only be suspected.

The writing symbols can be divided into a total of three categories:

1. So-called ideograms or word signs consist of the stylized representation of an object and contain no other sound value. Such images could stand as individual signs or be composed of two different signs.

2. Sound signs relate to the spoken sound value of a word. Thus some pictorial representations could be used to write other words that were associated with them on a higher level.

3. Determinatives were often added to picture words to make their relationship clear. Thus, for example, the sign for "city" was often added to the names of cities.

Only the signs that represented a deity represent real symbols in hieroglyphic writing.

HEIROGLYPHICS

1. The picture of the ointment jar stands for "fat," "oil," and "ointment." Such vessels traditionally received the seven sacred oils that were used in the cult of gods and burial. The Egyptians also liked to used ointments to keep their skin smooth in the dry desert climate.

2. Here, the sign for the ritual water vessel can be seen. It appears in connection with the drink offering and religious purification ceremonies.

3. This is one of the oldest hieroglyphics. It describes the word "city," in which a crossing of roads is shown within a fortified city wall.

4. The hieroglyphic of the pointed bread also stands for the verb "to give," since bread played a large role in sacrifice ceremonies.

5. The ideogram for "earth" relates to the fertile flood land along the Nile, consisting of the signs for island and three grains of sand.

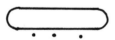

 6. The moon is represented either as a crescent or as a combination of the crescent moon (always horizontal) and the disk of the full moon.

7. Three stylized mountains stand for the hill land and the desert, and also represent foreign lands, since all areas outside the Nile valley were classified as foreign and enemy territory.

 8. The hieroglyphic for the word "sky" is a stylized representation of the sky goddess, Nut.

9. Legs walking to the right describe the word "come."

 10. Legs going in the direction toward the left reflect "return" or also "retreat."

1.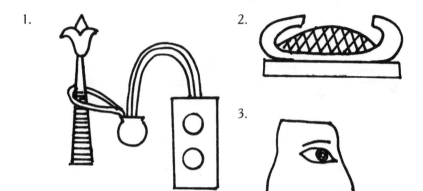

2.

3.

4.

5.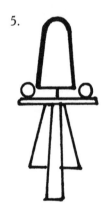

6.

7.

8.

HEIROGLYPHICS

1. The writing tools stand for the "writer" or the process of "writing."

2. The hieroglyphic for "fisher" consists of a stylized fishing boat together with a fishing net.

3. The picture of the nose embodies everything that has to do with the nose, the sense of smell, and joy. Since the breath of life enters through it, special importance was assigned to it. By striking the nose off a statue and carving out its name, people attempted to prevent hated contemporaries from living on after death.

4. The harp was the favorite musical instrument in ancient Egypt. Its players formed regular dynasties, in which musical ability was transmitted from parents to children.

5. The symbol for "east."

6. The hieroglyphic for "west" also denotes the peoples of the west.

7. Here, the written sign for "wind" can be seen.

8. The ideogram for "water."

1a

1b

1c

2a

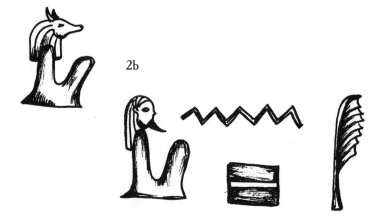

2b

Amun and Anubis in picture and sound writing

THE NAMES OF GODS

Signs of the god Amun.

1a. When Amun was represented as a heavenly body, a picture of the disk of the sun was sufficient to write his name.

1b. In many places, especially where deities with ram's heads were worshipped, the sign for Amun was composed of the symbols for "god" and "ram's head."

1c. When the name of the god was written in letters, the result was this picture with the sound value "amn" = Ammon/Amun.

Symbols of the god Anubis.

2a. The word sign for this god is characterized by a jackal's head, to which the universal symbol for "god" was added.

2b. In the method of writing sounds, these or similar hieroglyphics were used, which gave the sound value "anp." The pronunciation "Anubis" is quite certain, since contemporary writers of other peoples recorded the names of gods in their languages. It was their records that first made it at all possible to decipher the Egyptian hieroglyphics.

REGIONAL SIGNS

In the following, the 20 regional signs of Lower Egypt are listed. They represent the 20 agricultural regions and their governments. The symbols are found both on standards and also on the heads of regional gods with human form in the temples.

1. The sign for the capital city Heliopolis, with the meaning "undamaged scepter."

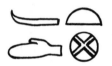

2. The throne site, Behdet, is represented by this regional sign written in letters.

3. Here, Anezti, the regional god of the land can be seen. The capital is Busiris.

4. The coat of arms of the capital city Memphis consists of the written signs for "wall" and "white."

42

5. The shield of the goddess Neith is combined with that of the rush for the southern region "Southern Shield."

6. In combination with the papyrus plant, the shield of Neith stands for the province "Northern Shield."

7. The capital city Bubastis of the region "Royal Child, Forward Region." The writing sign for "forward" is formed from three standing jars bound together.

8. The stylized harpoon next to the boat and the sign for "west" symbolized the western region.

9. The eastern region was represented by a boot with a harpoon and the sign for "east."

10. The coat of arms of the "Forward East Region" is composed of the standing jars (front) and the sign for "east."

11. The shape of a leg of beef, which was presented as an offering in early times, is borrowed as the coat of arms for the capital city Letopolis.

12. The "Heseb Bull" region.

13. The "black bull" is the sign for the capital city Athribis.

14. The capital city Sebennytos bears the signs "cow with calf."

15. The "Mountain Bull" region shows the hieroglyphics for "mountain" and "bull."

16. The crouching hawk is the holy animal of the regional god Sopdu, whose land bears the same name.

17 The signs "royal child" and "Rear Region" denote the capital city of lands of Tanis. The word "end" as a hieroglyphic was indicated by the hind end of an animal.

18. The written sign for "west" stands for the Western Region.

19. The capital city Hermopolis bore the sacred ibis as a heraldic animal.

20. The lepidotos fish was the symbol of the capital city Mendes, whose regional goddess Hatmehit was likewise represented by a fish on her head.

1.

2.

3.

spiral, cord, kheker

SPIRAL, CORD, AND KHEKER SIGNS

1. Spiral-shaped decorations are found on many objects from ancient Egypt. Originally, the shape was probably associated with a coiled snake. As a protective symbol on amulets, the spiral embodied the life line in the eternal cycle of birth and death. Also, this shape indicates the dynamics of further development that takes place as life cycles follow one another.

2. Cords are associated in both worldly and magical spheres with the state of being bound. The drawing shows Horus, who is holding the people of the land of the papyrus bushes by the cord of captivity. Ropes were often represented in the form of snakes when binding an enemy was involved. If amulets were made in the form of knotted ropes, this involved binding and protecting the magic contained in them.

3. The decorative kheker signs were painted on many temples and burial chambers. They point upward to the original home of the gods in prehistory, where in the beginning of time the gods ruled over the land.

THE MEANING OF COLORS

With the word "color," the "essence" of an object or creature is described at the same time. The coloring always related to characteristics of the persons represented. Thus in classical Egyptian art, male bodies were painted in strong brown colors, while women received a lighter, yellowish shade of color. Men received an orange color only when age and frailty were to be represented.

White: The color white was considered an expression of holiness and joy. It has been suggested that this color of purity was used for sacred objects and buildings. White symbolized cosmic power and pure divine light.

Black represented a kind of opposite to white, embodying the underworld. Thus a black pelt was also given to the Anubis, the god of death. This color was, for example, a symbol of the original ground to which all life must return in order to be reborn from it. On this basis, pictures of the fertility goddess Min were mostly painted with black colors, as a sign of rebirth.

Red: In ancient Egypt, red had a dual meaning. On the one hand, this color was valued for its stimulating, life-affirming radiation; on the other hand, it was associated with blood and rage, which was reminiscent of the ceremonies of sacrifice and death. Since the god Set had red hair and eyes, the color red came to express danger as this god was increasingly moved into the camp of the Evil One. Destruction was also attributed to Set, as red cattle, even people with a reddish skin tone in early times, were sacrificed.

In contrast to the color red, green stands for "good" in general. The color of vegetation and emerging new life promised protection and happiness. The green-skinned Osiris was also worshipped as the "great green one," a symbol of rebirth.

The color blue indicates the divine aspect of being. Thus the original god Amun was given the skin color blue as an expression of the endless cosmos. The other gods wore wigs and beards of blue color as an indication of their divine origin.

When combined, these two colors, blue and green, were considered a symbol of maturity. This is also the double crown, which was composed of the white crown (it actually consisted of a green reed) of Upper Egypt and the red crown of Lower Egypt, was seen as a sign of union and completeness.

DEITIES

1.

2.

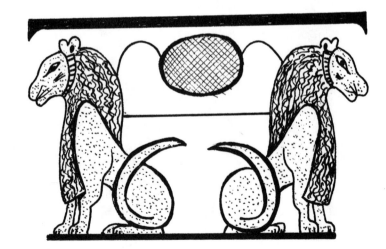

Amun and Aker

ORIGINAL GODS: AMUN AND AKER

1. The human-shaped god Amun involved a rather abstract original god. He was often associated with the breath of the wind, and in general his name meant "the Secluded One." He and his wife, Amaunet, constituted the original couple of the gods. In his appearance as a god of fertility, he was associated with the ram. But the goose and the snake were also assigned to him as sacred animals.

The god Amun should rather be seen as superordinate, as the soul of all being and things, as the sum of all existence.

In the New Kingdom, Amun was named in Thebes as the god of the kingdom, and he also received the aspect of the sun god, Re, and was called Amun-Re. His most important holy site is the temple system of Karnak, where he was worshiped with the moon child, Khensu, and the goddess Mut.

2. A strip of land with human or lion heads at its ends denoted the earth god Aker. This god bears the barque of the sun during its nightly journey through its dark realm. Aker's door wings, which were the entrance to the underworld, were guarded by the two lions. One animal looked toward the west, in the direction in which the kingdom of the dead lay and the sun started its night journey. The other lion looked toward the east, where the sun reappeared from the underworld.

1.

2.

3.

Anubis

GOD OF DEATH AND WATCHER OF MUMMIES: ANUBIS

In ancient Egypt, the jackal was often hated because of its shadow at graves. People hoped to be able to put an end to its activity by making it a god. Thus Anubis, the god of death, had the form of a dog or jackal. The nightly howling of the dogs among the graves likewise led to the assumption that the animals were protecting the dead during the night.

1. This wall painting shows Anubis, the protective god of mummies in human form with the head of a god. In imitation of this image, the priests who performed mummification wore jackal masks with painted clay, since the god was also considered a specialist in embalming. Originally, Anubis was the protector of mummies against evil power. In later times, when Osiris also functioned as god of the dead, he became a servant and from then on performed the weighing of the heart at the court of the dead.

Dogs and jackals were also kept as sacred animals of this god in buildings next to the temple, and they were embalmed and mummified after death.

2. The hieroglyphic for the god Anubis has the meaning "first among secrets." This god was represented here in animal form on a box full of secrets. The container presumably had something to do with the sarcophagus or with canopic jars, the containers in which the entrails were preserved.

3. A variant written form shows the god in human form with the head of a dog. This hieroglyphic can, however, also relate to one of the other gods with the form of a dog, such as Wepwawet, the god of Assiut, or Khontamenti of Abydos.

1.

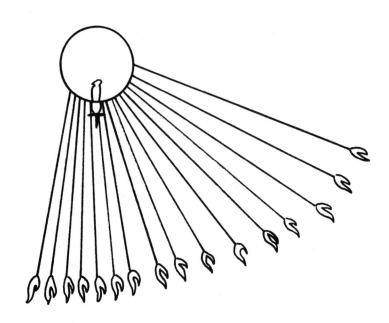

2.

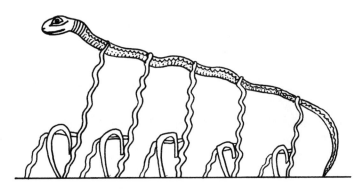

Aton and Apophis

THE POWER OF LIGHT AND DARKNESS: ATON AND APOPHIS

1. In the beginning, the disk of the sun was itself called Aton. Later, Aton was considered as an avatar of the sun god, Re, and was represented as a human with the head of a hawk. King Amenophis IV changed his name to Akhenaton ("beloved of Aton") and named Aton as the only deity. He had Aton represented as the sun disk with arms and hands and caused the symbol of the loop of life to be worn. Aton retained this image even after his reign.

2. The giant snake demon Apophis was considered the counterpart to the sun god and symbol of the dark powers. According to the myth, Apophis grasped the ship of the sun at sundown and sunrise. The blood of the injured demon thereby colored the sky red. Nevertheless, he kept trying to hold back the sun's journey, and every day he was again thrown down and defeated. Apophis was often equated with Set, the enemy of the gods and ruler of the destructive forces.

Atum

THE ORIGINAL CREATOR: ATUM

The god Atum, the creator god who arose from himself, was once worshiped in Heliopolis. He embodied the shapeless chaos of prehistory, the original ground from which all existence derived and to which everything will return. Thus, its image is found in connection with various natural phenomena and animals. According to the myth, Atum, with the help of his own female aspect by self-marriage, created the gods Shu (air) and Tefnut (fertility).

In the Book of the Dead, Atum said that he would one day destroy his creation and change himself back into the original snake. Later dynasties also connected this god with the origin of the monarchy and integrated him into the sun cycle. Here, he represented the god who ages every evening, goes down tired, and rises again on the next day.

Ba, the soul bird

SYMBOL OF SOUL POWER: BA

The god Ba represents the embodiment of the inescapable power of the soul. In ancient times, Ba was equated with the appearance and the spirit of a god. Thus, the phoenix of Heliopolis was the Ba of the god Re. Apis of Memphis is the Ba of Osiris. Kings had, in addition to their personal strengths, also the royal, divine Ba.

Only after the end of the Old Kingdom did this power become attributed to all people. The painters of the New Kingdom often show the Ba bird sitting on the trees that were planted near graves. It symbolizes mental powers that ruled the soul, spirit, and body and made it possible for the individual to manifest itself in any desired shape.

The hieroglyphic for the Ba (lower figure) represents an African stork and has the sound value "bz" or "b." It is generally translated incorrectly by the concept of "soul." In fact, its meaning is significantly broader, as can be seen in the description above. The representation of the Ba as a bird is understandable, since the Egyptians conceived themselves as flying to heaven after death as a bird, in order to exist further in another form.

1.

2.

Bastet and cat mummy

GODDESS IN CAT FORM: BASTET

In the Old Kingdom, representations of domesticated house cats are completely lacking. Instead, there are representations of wild cats, such as the cats of Heliopolis that killed the evil Apophis snake in the Book of the Dead. Only after the second millennium before Christ, did the cat find its place as house animals in the life of the ancient Egyptians. From then on, it was very popular and was under the protection of powerful taboos. After their death, the animals were carefully embalmed and deified. As the conqueror of Apophis, the cat was the sacred animal of the sun god. The male cat was considered to be his incarnation, and female cats were equated with the eye of the sun. Therefore, many cat figures wear a scarab on their head or breast as a symbol of the rising sun.

1. In the delta city Bubastis, the cat goddess Bastet was worshiped since the Old Kingdom as a gentle form of the lion-headed goddess Sekhmet. Her sacred animal was the tan-colored cat. Bastet was considered to be the mother of the lion god Miysis, who had the title "lord of the massacre." So it was also forbidden to go hunting for lions on the feast day of this goddess. Although it was originally represented as having a lion's head, its facial features grew softer and more friendly over time, until Bastet finally became the positive half of the being Sekhmet. From this time on, Bastet appeared as a female figure with the head of a cat or in the form of a sitting cat (Fig. 1). From then on, it governed the women's pleasant, domestic sphere, including love and happiness.

2. The mummy of a Bastet cat was from the late period, which was carefully wrapped in several layers of narrow linen strips.

The protective spirit Bes

PROTECTIVE SPIRIT IN DWARF FORM: BES

Especially among simple peoples, the shape of the Bes was very popular as a domestic protective god. He stood as a representative of a whole series of benevolent gnomelike beings, who protected the private sphere and warded off malevolent demons. Their clothing almost soley consisted of a lion or panther pelt that they wore on their backs. During the 18th Dynasty, however, winged forms of the Bes are also found. This spirit is also represented with the sa loop (shown at upper left) as a symbol of protection, and he carries various objects with him that are connected with his particular tasks. Knives serve to ward off demons and dangerous animals. Musical instruments were to make the gods favorable and to please them, and on the other hand to drive away evil demons. One particular aspect of the Bes was called Aha, which means "fighter." It can often be seen in battle with snakes or gazelles belonging to Set.

Originally, the dwarf being was responsible for the period of childbirth and had to protect houses from dangerous animals. In later periods, his field of activity expanded to many household objects. Thus, representations of the Bes are found on pillows, in order to protect sleep, and on mirrors and cosmetic articles, in order to ward off the Evil Eye. His inclusion with followers of Hathor, who was responsible for feminine beauty, among other things, becomes clear in this way.

1.

2.

Khnemu

GOD OF FERTILITY AND CREATION: KHNEMU

1. The ram-headed god Khnemu is shown in his capacity as god of creation, creating a prince and his ka with the aid of his potter's wheel. From one of the figures he forms the physical body of the new person, which he sends into the mother's womb as semen. The other figure is created as the person's ka; it is his purer, immortal part, which is born with him. Khnemu, together with the frog-headed god Heket, was considered as an assistant in childbirth. This god was worshiped as the creator of all being especially in the southern Egyptian city Esne. Since he combined several ram deities in his form, he was sometimes given four heads, to symbolize his four spheres of power: sky, air, earth, and underworld.

As far back as the old period, Khnemu had the form of a ram, and he only received his human form toward the end of the Old Kingdom. His task as watcher of the source of the Nile also included controlling the flood water in order to ensure rich harvests and end famines.

Khnemu's ram shape derives from a breed of sheep that died out in Egypt in ancient times. In the Necropolis of sacred rams in Elephantine, countless animals were mummified and placed in gilded sarcophagi.

2. This ideogram shows how the god Khnemu is written, but he can also be written as a standing ram.

Khensu

THE MOON CHILD: KHENSU

Typical of representations of the moon child, Khensu, is the mummified form with closed legs and side lock, which characterize him as a youth. This sculpture shows the Theban god with the insignia of rulership, scourge and crook, in his hands. The head-covering in the form of the moon disk crescent, which is otherwise common, is missing here. Khensu was the child of Amun and Mut and was called "the Wanderer," since he wandered through the sky at night. As the sun of the night, he was sometimes also represented with the head of a hawk.

Khensu was highly revered by the people, mainly as an oracle god and as a protector from diseases. Thus, some wall paintings show him accompanying Horus, standing on crocodiles. In the subordinate sense, he was considered to be the moon child, that is, an aspect of the young Horus.

Such associations were based on the thinking of the Egyptians about the higher recognition that time cannot be defined in the form of a straight line, but that in the end all events occur simultaneously. Therefore, it was possible to invoke the various age aspects of a god, like partial personalities, at any time.

Tuatmutef, Qebhsennuf, Mesthi, and Hapi

VESSELS FOR PRESERVING THE ENTRAILS: TUATMUTEF, QEBHSENNUF, MESTHI, AND HAPI

Four canopic jars that contained the entrails of the deceased were buried with each body. Like the mummies themselves, the internal organs were also carefully embalmed, which was absolutely necessary for the resurrection of the dead. The vessels embodied the four sons of Horus and were to accompany the dead into the heavenly realm, since they also represent the four celestial directions. In addition, they were to protect the person who had been buried from hunger and thirst, because they preserved the organs involved.

Mesthi, who had human shape, stood for the south and bore the stomach and intestines. Tuatmutef, jackal-headed guardian of the east, watched the deceased person's heart and lungs. Qebhsennuf received the liver and gall bladder, which were wrapped in bandages. He is the hawk-headed son of a god. The protector of the smaller organs, Hapi, bore the head of a monkey.

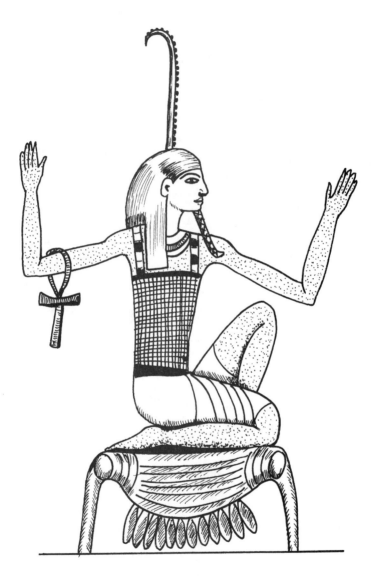

Heh

GOD OF ETERNITY: HEH

The kneeling god Heh can be seen here on the sign for "gold," which represents an embodiment of innumerable amounts. The hieroglyphic that shows his form then stands also for the number "million."

His attribute is the cut palm branch, which symbolizes the annual calendar and should indicate countless years of happiness for the king's reign. As an embodiment of "many," this god appears only seldom as a separate individual, but usually forms a group with other Heh's. They jointly indicate a kind of multiplication of the air god Shu and have the endless aspect of that god. Heh is the endlessness of time and is always represented with raised arms as a sky-bearer.

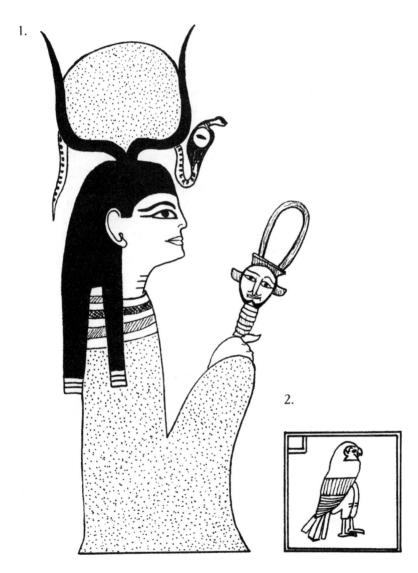

1.

2.

Hathor

GODDESS OF THE HEAVENLY DEPTHS: HATHOR

The cult of the goddess Hathor was widespread and went far back to pre-dynastic times. Originally, she was worshiped as the heavenly cow, the original mother, and heavenly food-giver. As an embodiment of complete femininity, the original goddess later received the form of a woman, to whom only the horns of the cow and the ears of the cow, were assigned. Dendera was originally the main site of the cult of Hathor, where she was worshiped as "female soul with the two faces." She was considered to be the goddess of the dead in Thebes, where the last wish of a dying person included being protected from the powers of darkness as a follower of Hathor. Before Isis replaced this original deity, Hathor was considered to be the mother of Horus. Later, she served as the embodiment of the all-encompassing heavenly depths.

1. This wall painting shows Hathor in human form with an ankh bearing the face of Osiris in her hand. Here, this involves a representation from the 20th Dynasty. In the earthly sphere, Hathor was also the goddess of the dance, love, and drunkenness.

2. The hieroglyphic for this goddess shows a hawk inside a palace wall, because the name Hathor means "house of Horus," and relates to its meaning as the source of the sky, in which the divine hawk lives.

1.

2.

Horus

SKY GOD: HORUS

1. This bronze figure from the 26th Dynasty shows the sky god Horus in human form with the head of a hawk. In ancient times, the hawk was worshiped throughout the land as a divine manifestation. Its lust for battle and its flying ability made the hawk become the king of the gods in the end. The various local deities were merged into the trans-regional god Horus, the sky hawk. This god symbolized the sky; the sun and the moon were his eyes. He combined the characteristics of a sky god with those of a dynasty god and founder of the Egyptian Kingdom. Thus, the pharaoh was an incarnation of Horus and embodied an aspect of this god. From a early on, the name of the hawk god was an element of the royal title. The sign for "king" shows a hawk in a rectangle, which symbolizes the palace walls.

In ancient times, Horus was considered to be the brother of his rival, Set. After he lost an eye in battle with him, the gods agreed to divide his rulership of the Nile land. Thus Horus became the lord over Lower Egypt and Set became the land god of Upper Egypt. In later times, Set was driven out of his realm and was considered to be only the ruler of the barren desert and the barbaric peoples, while Horus was worshiped as the highest god of all Egypt. In the time when the cult of Osiris flourished, Horus was considered to be the son of Osiris and nephew of Set. As the avenger and heir of his father, he now led a bitter battle against his brother, Set, from which he emerged as the victor.

2. The written sign for this god shows a stylized hawk and also stands for the general concept of "god."

Isis and Nephthys

SISTERS OSIRIS: ISIS AND NEPHTHYS

1. This ornament shows the grieving goddesses Nephthys (left) and Isis (right.) They protect the tet pillar, the amulet of Osiris, with their wings. Nephthys is, like Isis, Osiris, and Set, a child of Geb and Nut. In accordance with the dualistic world view of the Egyptians, the "positive" and fertile couple Isis and Osiris: contrasted with the "negative," essentially barren couple Nephthys and Set. The form of the goddess Nephthys herself is not negative, however, since she is mourning her murdered brother

Osiris with her sister. Nephthys means "lady of the house," but almost nothing is known of her essential characteristics. She involves a new creation, probably out of the need give a wife to Set. The name Isis is identical with the name for "throne." Originally she was considered to be the symbolic mother of all kings and the embodiment of the occupant of the throne. According to the myth, she was the sister and wife (a thoroughly common connection in the Egyptian royal houses) of Osiris and gave birth to their son Horus. She protected him, and thereby also human children, from predators and other dangers. Isis was also considered to be full of magic, since she blew new life breath into the dead Osiris. This goddess was generally represented in human shape, bearing the symbol of the throne on her head. In her function as protectress, she had wings, and in some cases she was represented with her sister Nephthys as a harrier (bird of prey). Later, in the New Kingdom, the form of the goddess Isis was often blended with that of the original goddess Hathor, in which process she took over her signs, the cow horns and the sun disk.

2.

2. Here, the hieroglyphic for the goddess Nephthys is shown. Her name was represented in human form, as here, or only in the form of her head covering.

3. This ideogram stands for the word "throne" or "seat" and is the identifying sign of the goddess Isis. She is usually represented with this sign on her head.

Joh

JOH

The god Joh represented an embodiment of the moon. As a symbol, he carried the moon signs, the disk and the crescent, on his head. Only seldom did this original god appear in human form. In most documents and pictures, he was reduced to the manifestation of the heavenly bodies that are also his symbol. This moon sign was worn as an ornament by the moon child, Khensu.

In ancient Egypt, the moon was the son of the night and thus the right eye of Horus. The deities Osiris, Thoth, and later also the goddess Isis were considered to be his protectors. The continual moon cycles were interpreted as an indication of death and resurrection. Its phases were also associated with the fourteen days of the dismemberment of Osiris, the period of the waning moon. From their relationships, it is understandable that the crescent (sickle) moon can also appear in pictures and texts by a cutting weapon (with Thoth) or a leg, as a relic of Osiris.

Maat

PROTECTRESS OF THE COSMIC ORDER: MAAT

As with most of the human-shaped deities of Egypt, the goddess Maat also involves an abstraction. She represents an embodiment of the cosmic order, to which the gods, the kings, and the people were subject. Since she was responsible for the cyclic nature of life, no existence was conceivable without her actions.

The judge of the state was at the same time the priest of Maat, since she embodied the seat of being, right, truth, and the world order. Her symbol of truth was the feather, as an expression of lightness, including proper and correct behavior. Thus the heart of a person should also not weigh more than a feather on the scale of the divine court.

The cult of the goddess Maat related primarily to the standards and laws of Egyptian society and controlled the relationships between pharaohs and subjects. Thus the king rewarded obedience by his subjects and had to assure a harmonious relationship to the gods through fulfillment of his religious duties. In this way, he supported the gods in their tasks of maintaining the cosmic balance, on which both the existence of the deities and also that of the people depended.

1.

2.

3.

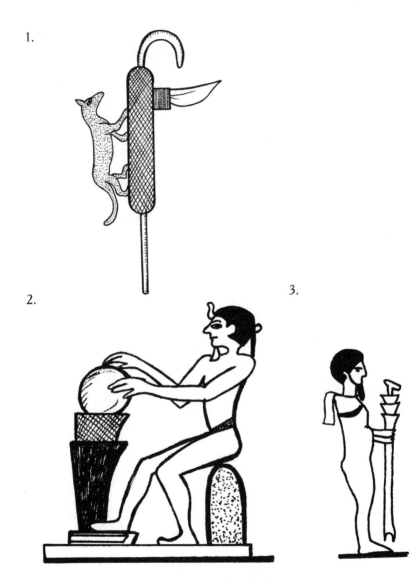

Maftet and Ptah

GODS OF JUSTICE AND CREATIVE POWER: MAFTET AND PTAH

1. The goddess Maftet runs in the form of a cat-shaped animal up the staff of an execution device. At the side, there is a coil of rope, which holds a knife. In later times, Maftet also played a significant role in the court of the otherworld. Her principal task consisted of combating sins and snakes.

2. The picture shows Ptah as the creator of the earth, as he is creating life on a potter's wheel. He was the city god of Memphis, as well as the god of crafts and creativity. His power is related to the heart and the tongue, since his words allow the world to be formed and his heartbeat continually provides energy and life force to creation.

3. In Ptah's scepter are united the tet column and uas. His head is always covered with a smooth blue cap. Ptah, the ancient one, is always represented in human form, and his body is mostly covered with a narrow, long, ceremonial robe that shows only his hands and head. He is mainly portrayed standing.

1.

2.

3.

4.

Min

GOD OF FERTILITY: MIN

1. The god Min was the god of both animal and plant fertility. The relief represented here shows him in his typical manifestation in the form of a mummy with one arm raised and erect phallus.

Min was one of the most important fertility gods of the Nile land. His origin is disputed, however, and probably came from abroad, possibly Eritrea, or even in the fabled kingdom of Punt. In the old texts, he was clearly called the "black-skinned one" and a foreigner.

2. His divinity was often identified by the sign of the round hut.

3. Occasionally, it was respresented by the lettuce bed, which was considered to be an aphrodisiac.

4. In ancient times, this god was worshiped in a fetish resembling a bundle of lightning.

Menthu

GOD OF WAR: MENTHU

This relief shows the hawk-headed god of war, Menthu, who is holding his attributes, the sickle sword and the loop of life. As identification, he wore the sun disk and two high feathers on his head. The principal site of his cult was Thebes, and in Karnak today, there are still the remains of his temple. During periods of war of the Theban Dynasty, this god nearly became the god of the dynasty, since the struggle for reunification of the Egyptian kingdom was waged under his patronage. After the conquest, he retained the position of warlord, while Amun replaced him as the highest deity.

The task of the god Menthu consisted of killing the enemies of his father, Re, with a spear. Bulls and hawks were the animals that were considered to be his manifestations on the earth. In addition, he was assigned a white animal with a black face, which was called Bukhis.

In the New Kingdom, Menthu changed into the protective spirit of the king, by whose side he stood in sporting contests and in battle.

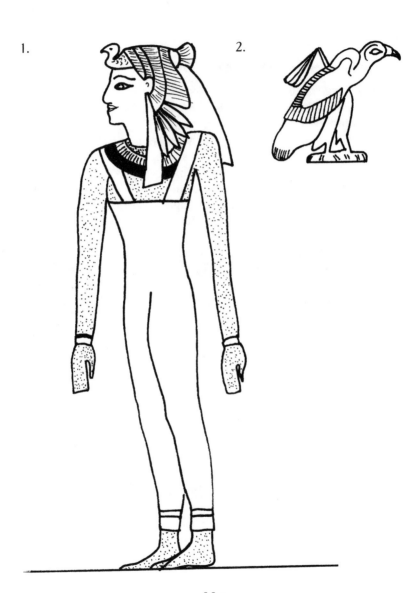

1.　　　　　2.

Mut

THE ORIGINAL MOTHER: MUT

1. The usual representation of the goddess Mut is as the wife of Amun and mother of the moon child, Khensu. In Thebes, these three deities were worshiped as a triad.

Almost always, this goddess wore on her head as identification a vulture headdress, the traditional head ornament of queens. She embodies here mainly the aspect of the queen as a mother, since Mut involves integration of the pre-historical mother goddess. Many other female goddesses therefore also wore the symbolic vulture headdress on their heads. In connection with the Theban triad, Mut stood for the institution of the family and its protection.

In the New Kingdom, after Amun had been named the sun god, Mut again became the original mother, called mother of the sun.

2. The hieroglyphic of the goddess Mut the vulture, which stands for the vulture headdress. The picture of the goddess herself was, in contrast, always in human form with the headdress or a combination of vulture and crown on her head.

Nekhebet

LAND GODDESS OF UPPER EGYPT: NEKHEBET

The vulture goddess Nekhebet was originally worshiped in the Upper Egyptian locality Elkab. After the unification with the neighboring city of Neken to become the capital of Upper Egypt, she became the protectress of the land. The vulture became the symbolic animal of this half of the land, while Lower Egypt was represented by the snake of the goddess Buto. Both protective goddesses can sometimes be viewed also as the mythical mother of the king, to whom she offers her breasts.

In royal heraldry, Nekhebet was mainly seen in her vulture form, and her image was worn by the queens in the shape of the vulture headdress as a crown. The uraeus snake of the royal crown represented her counterpart here as well.

In the New Kingdom and in later times, the simple people prayed to this goddess also as the goddess of birth, and she was often shown in this characteristic in human form with the skin of a vulture on her head.

1.

2.

Nefertem

THE SUN CHILD: NEFERTEM

1. The child god Nefertem was mostly represented sitting on a lotus leaf, sucking his thumb or a flower. He wore the child's side lock as his hairstyle. He was the son of the lion-headed goddess Sekhmet and the god Ptah. Therefore, lion-headed variants of the sun child are also encountered. His cult was mainly centered in Memphis, where he was part of the sacred triad.

Nefertem was considered to be the embodiment of the original lotus and was described as the flower in the nose of Re, with whom he spent every day. The solar relationship allowed him to appear as the sun child, and his equivalence with the lotus blossom identified him as the god of fragrance.

2. This is the hieroglyphic of Nefertem.

1.

2.

3.

Neith

GODDESS OF WAR: NEITH

1. The protectress of the city Sais was the war goddess Neith. Her presence was identified by weapons, such as bows, arrows, and shields. Sculptures in the form of Neith and her weapons, arranged around the sarcophagus, were to protect the remains. In ancient times, she was considered to be the mother of the crocodile god Sebek.

The picture shows Neith in her function as dynasty god with the red crown of Lower Egypt. After an absence of almost two thousand years, her cult was revived in the 26th Dynasty, where she appeared in the form of an original goddess as mother god of Re. From then on, she was considered to be the original seed, from which both gods and people came into being. In her new androgynous position, she was identified as father of fathers and mother of mothers, and partly also as the Anima (feminine aspect of the soul) of the original god of creation, Khnemu.

In the cult of the dead, Neith came to be the protector of mummy bandages, whereby she was also named the lady of weaving.

2. The hieroglyphic for Neith was generally interpreted as a stylized picture of two bows bound together and characterized the goddess as protectress of bows.

3. The other symbol of this goddess, which represents a shield over which two arrows cross, was called hemesut. It was viewed as an independent being, as the embodiment of the female creative and life force, and formed a female counterpart to the male ka.

1.

2.

Nut, Shu and Geb

THE GODS OF THE AIR AND THE SKY: NUT, SHU, AND GEB

1. The goddess Nut is the vault of heaven personified. She was the daughter of the air god, Shu, who supports his stretched body from below. Her hands and feet touch the east and west points of the horizon. In Figure 1 her newborn son is climbing up her leg in the form of a beetle. The setting sun, which is provided with wings, is found in front of her mouth. Nut was viewed as the mother of all heavenly bodies, including the sun god, Re. Every day, she swallows the heavenly bodies, in order to bear them again from her womb. She was represented many times as a nursing mother sow, as a "sow feeding her piglets."

Since Nut is a symbol of rebirth, burial chambers and sarcophagi were often decorated with her image.

2. The air god, Shu separated the sky god, Nut, from the earth god, Geb. This treatment symbolizes duality, the separation of the world into opposites, above and below, light and dark, good and evil. The barque of the sun, which is identified by the ram's head in the sun disk, can be seen in the sky. The god Shu is mostly represented as a man. Only in his function as a fighter and defender of the sun god does he sometimes receive a lion's head. In Egyptian mythology, Shu arrived as breath from the nose of the original god, Atum, together with his sister and wife, Tefnut, the moist air. The first pair of cosmic elements then created the sky goddess, Nut, and the earth god, Geb, who in turn created the gods Isis, Osiris, Nephthys, and Set. The ostrich feather, symbol of the god Shu, is symbolic of lightness and emptiness. Fog and clouds are Shu's elements, and they are often called his bones. Because of his position between the sky and the earth, he was also called the god of the wind.

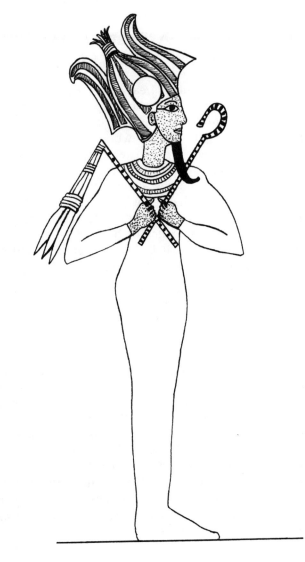

Osiris

GOD OF THE UNDERWORLD: OSIRIS

In general, the god of the dead, Osiris, is represented in the form of a mummy, holding a scepter and flail in his hands. His head is decorated with a feathered helmet crown. Osiris is one of the best known Gods of Egypt. He was the son of the sky goddess, Nut, and the earth god, Geb. Lordship over the earth was transferred to him by his father. The myth further tells that Osiris attracted the envy of Set, after he introduced grape-growing and farming. At this time, this god also received the name Wennofer, which means "the good being" or "the complete one." Tempted by overpowering jealousy, his brother, Set, drowned him in the Nile. This death in water was associated with the annual flooding of the Nile, which made a new harvest possible. Legends of the dismemberment of Osiris derived from a later period, after several places claimed to own his body parts. Thus Abydos claimed the head, Busiris the spine (Tet pillar), Philae a bone, and Mendes the penis of the God. The body parts were buried in graves, and a tree was planted next to each of them as a sign of resurrection. The myths tell how Osiris's sister and wife, the goddess Isis, reassembled these parts after a long search. He owed his resurrection to Anubis's art of embalming and the loving Isis, who breathed the breath of life into him with her wings. His son, Horus, embraced him and gave him the Horus eye to eat. Since then, this god became the symbol of the resurrection. When Horus restored the order that had been destroyed by occupying the throne as sun god, Osiris became the son of the night, since the moon embodied the cyclical renewal of life.

The colors of Osiris are white, like the mummy bandages, and black, as the color of death. His skin is green, like plants. He had adopted the crook and flail, the signs of his rulership, from the original deity Anezti of Busiris, whose place he assumed.

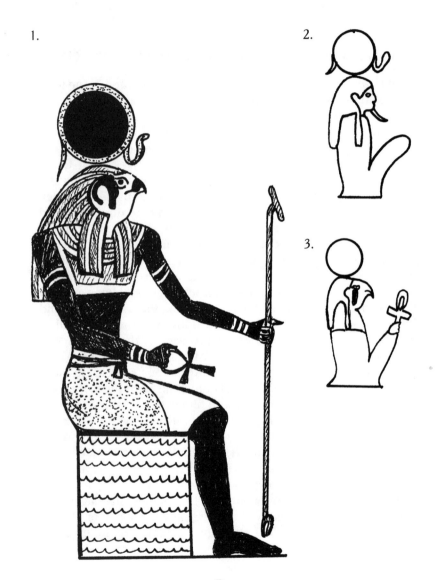

Re

THE SUN GOD: RE

1. The sun was viewed as the visible body of the sun god, Re. At the time of the first five dynasties, Re was worshiped as a purely cosmic deity in the form of the sun disk. Only later, with the increasing popularity of the hawk god, Horus, did he assumed his human form and the hawk's head; he bears the sun disk on this head as an unmistakable sign. From then on, he came to be seen as a link between worlds, who crossed the sky ocean in his sun barque together with his daughter, Maat, who was responsible for the cosmic order, and the ibis god, Thoth, his vizier.

2. This hieroglyphic shows the usual way of writing the name Re. The beard indicates that he is a ruler, and the divine cobra is coiled around the sun disk on his head.

3. Another frequent way of writing it shows the god with the head of a hawk. This derives from a later period. In the beginning, Re was represented only as a round sun disk.

Sekhmet

GODDESS OF WAR AND DESTRUCTION: SEKHMET

The lion goddess Sekhmet probably became the wife of Ptah, to whom she was a kind of opposite, only because the sites of their cults were close to each other. She appeared in the form of a lion or of a woman with the head of a lion. Sekhmet, whose name means "the powerful one," accompanied the ruler into war, and at times she was even called the mother of the ruler. In her furious aspect, she was even superior to the followers of Set and the Apophis snake. Her weapons were the hot desert wind and arrows, which she shot into the hearts of her enemies. In this way, Sekhmet also became the fire-breathing Uraeus and thus the eye of Re. In her infinite fury, she also spread fear and fright through diseases and plagues. If her wrath could be appeased, however, she became "full of magic," and bore the additional name Werethekau. In this characteristic, she used her power for healing and in this way accelerated the restoration of order in the kingdom. For this reason, physicians were also called "priests of Sekhmet."

Sekhmet was worshiped in Memphis as the wife of Ptah and mother of their son, Nefertem. After Thebes was named as the new capital, she united the goddess Mut, who resided there, with the lioness as Mut-Sekhmet. The goddess Hathor could also assume the aspect of Sekhmet at times.

1.

2.

3.

Serqet

SERQET: PROTECTING GODDESS OF LIFE

1. Together with Isis, Neith, and Nephthys, the goddess Serqet formed the protective foursome who guarded the dead. The scorpion goddess was one of the magical beings that accompanied the sun god in battle with their magical powers against his enemies. Since the earliest times, the scorpion was considered to be a powerful symbol that protected against disaster, and she was therefore placed in the graves of kings.

Among the followers of this goddess there was also a whole series of specialists who were involved with dangerous consequences and healing scorpion bites. Her old name, Serqet-betu can be translated "the one who gives breath to throat." Since the breath was seen as the connection with life, Serqet was named the protectress of life.

2. The written sign for this goddess shows a stylized scorpion.

3. As a variant, this headless form, without the poison stinger, is often seen is burial chambers. In this way, the danger of this animal was driven away, since it was believed pictorial representations could be animated magically.

Seshat

GODDESS OF THE ART OF WRITING AND FATE: SESHAT

The goddess Seshat, "the one who stands before the house of books," is clearly recognizable by her head ornament, which consists of a seven-rayed star with a sickle-shaped frame. Her name is often written with this symbol. In pictures, she usually carries a stylus, a writing slate, or a palm rib in her hand and a panther skin over her robe.

Seshat was the goddess of the art of writing and calculation. Her task consisted of writing the royal annals, counting the regnal years of the pharaohs, and must be present at the jubilee feasts as a goddess. She is also at coronation ceremonies as the goddess of fate. Thus she assumed the position of the divine record-keeper. Another of Seshat's tasks was to lay the foundations of a new temple to be constructed by the hands of her priests.

GOD OF CHAOS AND DESTRUCTION: SET

1.

Set

Cosmic and social disorder were generally associated with the field of activities of the god Set (Fig. 1), whose most common additional name was "great in power." This god was usually presented in this form, as a man with the head of the mythical animal set. Originally, Set was the land god of Upper Egypt. After the unification of the two lands, however, he was pushed out to the barren regions. Many wall paintings show him in battle with the Apophis snake, standing at the bow of the sun barque. The mythical Set animals often pulled the sun barque instead of the usual jackals.

In the religious thinking of Egypt, life was played out between the opposing poles of good and evil, forces of creation and destruction. In this worldview, Set always embodied dark, destructive, and chaotic power. Thus the murderous sea and unpredictable storms were subject to him. In the animal kingdom, the donkey, antelope, pig, crocodile, hippopotamus, and fish were assigned to him. As the ruler over metals, iron ores were depicted as his bones.

With the spread of the cult of Osiris, Set became increasingly explained as the god of vegetation. As the myth told it, this god had lost his testicles in battle with the god Horus, and his fate was sealed as ruler of the barren desert regions. Since he also was assigned power over all non-Egyptian lands, he was seen during times of foreign rule as the embodiment of all evil and was regarded as an enemy of the state.

2.

2. The written sign for the god Set can be seen here.

3.

3. This hieroglyphic shows the mythical set animal, which probably represents a chimera, that is, a mixture of various kinds of animals. The erect tail and the angular, raised ears are typical. The sign stands for several expressions, all connected with destruction or violence. Among the inhabitants of the barren regions, this animal was a messenger of disaster, while among the nomadic tribes of Upper Egypt, it embodied the power of the regents.

Seker

PROTECTIVE GOD OF THE NECROPOLIS OF MEMPHIS: SEKER

Seker was represented as a hawk in a specially shaped barque that ends in an antelope head facing backward. In his original form, he was probably worshiped as a fertility god, since his image in ancient times was still drawn on a sled on fields, while participants in processions decorated themselves with wreaths of onions. In later times, however, other aspects were intertwined with this god. Since the site of his cult was located at the necropolis of Memphis, he became its protective god. According to the myth, he was the sky hawk, who lived in a secret cave in the kingdom of the dead. At this time, he was considered to be the protective lord of the forge.

After he was associated with the gods Osiris and Ptah in later times, he lost most of his individuality.

Tefnut

GODDESS OF THE LIFE-GIVING DEW: TEFNUT

The goddess Tefnut was created by the self-created original god, Atum, at the beginning of time, together with her brother, Shu. Tefnut was the goddess of moisture. She, along with Shu, formed the first pair of cosmic elements. From this pair of siblings came the opposing forces of the male and female principles.

As the god Atum became Re over the course of time, Shu and Tefnut were made into his children. From then on, they were also called the eyes of the sky lord, the sun and the moon. Tefnut was equated with the moon eye and received the additional name "lady of the flame," which relates to the power of moisture over fire.

Tefnut is a good example of the confusing multiplicity of Egyptian moon gods. The female aspect, with its power over the element of water, can be seen in the original goddess Tefnut.

1.

2.

3.

Thoth

THE LORD OF THE WORLD: THOTH

1. Worship of the ibis-headed god Thoth began in the region of the Nile Delta. The homeland of the ibis, embodied by this god's shape, was also there. Later, the Middle Egyptian city Hermopolis became the center of his cult. Here, he was also connected with the peacock god, Hez-ur, whose form he sometimes assumed. Like the monkey god, who also had his seat there, he was also considered to be the lord of the world, since the curved beak of the ibis was associated with the crescent of the moon. In the temple of the ibis cult, countless mummies of the sacred bird were found, which were also symbols of bliss. Since he was also considered to be the protective patron of writers, he was often portrayed with writing implements or a palm rib.

According to the tales, Thoth arose from the head of Set, who had swallowed a seed from the sun god Horus. As the radiating moon, this god came out of the dark power of Set and became the lord of time. In the sky of the gods of ancient Egypt, he was assigned the role of messenger of the gods.

2. This hieroglyphic shows the most common way of writing the god Thoth.

3. As a variant, the god can be seen in this written form as an ibis-headed man.

Taurt

PROTECTIVE DEMON OF PREGNANT WOMEN: TAURT

The goddess Taurt was a mixture of a female hippopotamus and a crocodile. In addition, she was provided with human arms and hanging breasts, which give her a kind and sometimes cheerful appearance. Taurt arose from the folk belief of the simple people and is therefore found less often in the representations of the glorious temples. The field of activity of this protective goddess related mainly to the family environment, especially to pregnancy, birth, and labor. In some pictures, she holds the sa loop in her hands as a symbol of life or a torch, to drive the evil powers away. In the drawing on the opposite page, she is holding a life-saving belt as used by fishermen at that time.

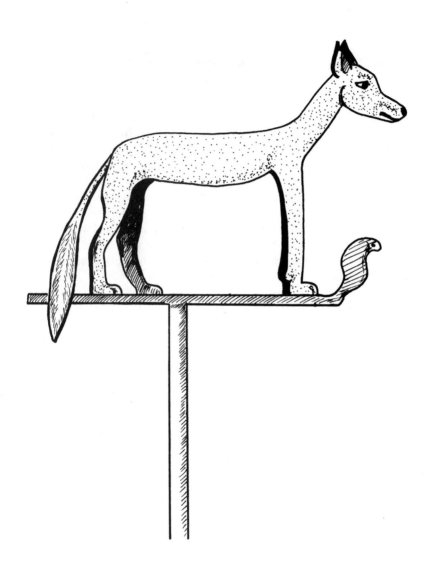

Wepwawet

DEITY OF WAR AND DEATH : WEPWAWET

The standard on the opposite page shows an image of the god Wepwawet. In general, he was represented as a black wolf or jackal and wascarried on such standards in processions. As the "path opener," he was carried at the head of the royal procession in ceremonies. He guaranteed victory by going into battle at the front. He was identified as a war god by a club and bow. Uniting both aspects, he also preceded the god Osiris, in order to clear all obstacles from the path. The form of Wepwawet is therefore also found in paintings in burial chambers, in which he is carried before the body in the procession. He was later placed on a standard, where he would keep watch over the deceased. The main site of the cult of this god was the city of Assiut, which was later renamed Lycopolis by the Greeks, who borrowed from the wolf-like form of the god.

Watcher demon

BEINGS OF DARKNESS: DEMONS

The picture shows a watcher in the form of a demon, who is protecting the gate to the underworld. In Egyptian mythology, demons were generally added to the deities. They often took on the task of executioner. For example, when the deceased had not withstood the test before the court of the otherworld, since they lived from evildoers, the demons drank their blood. The god Osiris alone was served by forty-two demonic judges of the dead and many watchers on the paths and at the gates to the underworld. They can be recognized by the signs of their power, such as snakes, knives, sparks, and scepters. The female demon monster Ammit, who ate the deceased sinners, should also be mentioned here. It had the body of a wildcat, the nose of a crocodile, and the rear end of a hippopotamus.

In the realm of the living, the beings of darkness, who were usually associated with Set, were connected with all kinds of disasters. Thus, they were made responsible for breakouts of diseases and wars. The people attempted to drive these beings away by beating them with branches or lighting torches.

In contrast to the malevolent demons, however, good demons, such as Bes and Taurt, were also invoked by the simple people. These deities also moved about in the shadow realm of Set, but they were benevolent to humans.

Identifying signs of the gods
Uaset, Amentet, Meret, Shu/Maat, and Seshat

IDENTIFYING SIGNS OF THE GODS, I

1. Uaset, goddess of the Thebes region, wears this scepter on her head. It consists of the regional sign (base), from which a ribbon and a feather arise.

2. The sign of Amentet represents a kind of embodiment of the west. The hieroglyphic for "west" can also be found in this form.

3. and 4. In Lower Egypt, the Nile God Meret wore a crown of papyrus stems (3); in Upper Egypt, lilies (4) were assigned to him.

5. The stylized ostrich feather identified both the air god Shu and also the goddess Maat, who stood for justice and world order.

6. Seshat, the goddess of the art of writing, wears this kind of seven- or five-pointed star on her head. It stands for learning and inspiration.

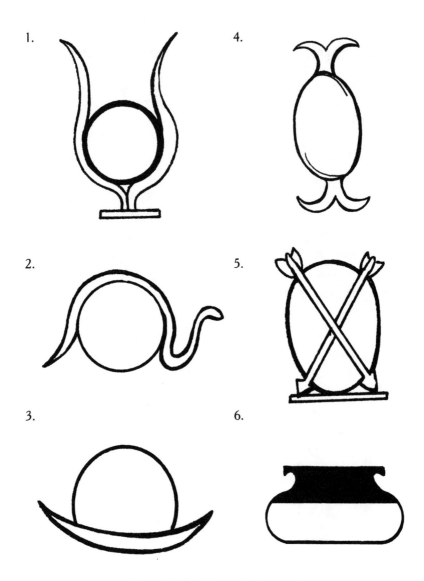

1.

4.

2.

5.

3.

6.

Identifying signs of the gods
Hathor, Harakhte, Khensu, Neith, Hemesut, and Nut

IDENTIFYING SIGNS OF THE GODS, II

1. The sun disk with the cow horns is the head ornament of the goddess Hathor, the mother of the sun god Horus. Later, in the New Kingdom, Isis took over this symbol from Hathor and appeared instead of her to a great extent. She was worshiped as the sister and wife of Osiris and mother of Horus.

2. Harakhte, the god of the morning sun, is represented with a hawk's head and wears a sun disk with uraeus snakes on his head. This sign is also associated with the war goddess Sekhmet, for whom the fire-breathing uraeus is likewise a symbol.

3. The moon god Khensu, the counselor, was identified with the moon disk and moon crescent.

4. Here, the symbol for the war goddess Neith can be seen. Additional insignia of her power are the shield, bow, and arrows. Since she is also the protectress of weaving, her signs were associated with a weaver' shuttle.

5. The shield with two crossed arrows identifies the protective goddess Hemesut.

6. The goddess Nut is the embodiment of the vault of heaven and is represented with round vessels and vulture wings. She is considered to be the mother of the sun god, Re, whom she swallows in the evening and gives birth to them again in the morning.

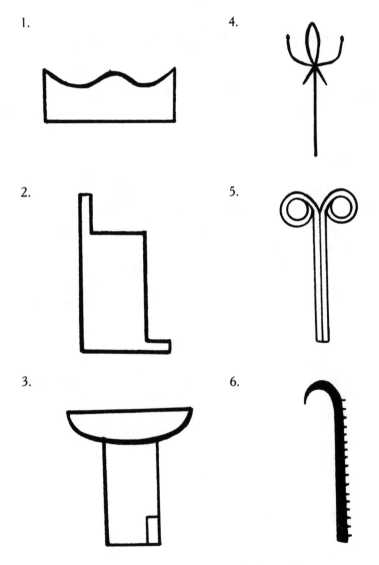

Identifying signs of the gods
Ha, Isis, Nephthys, Eiebt, Meshkent, and Heh

IDENTIFYING SIGNS OF THE GODS, III

1. This hieroglyphic for "desert" identifies Ha, the god of the western desert, as a head ornament.

2. The goddess Isis often wears this kind of hieroglyphic, which means "throne," on her head.

3. The head ornament of the goddess Nephthys consists of the hieroglyphic for "lady of the house.Nephthys is the daughter of the Geb and Nut and the wife of Set.

4. Eiebt, the personified east, wears this sign, which also finds use as a written symbol.

5. The headdress of the goddess Meshkent consists of a split stem, rolled up on both sides. It is incorporated into the child-bearing bricks, which served as foot supports during childbirth. This goddess formed the ka (life force) already in the mother's body and pronounced its fight at the time of birth.

6. Heh, the embodiment of endlessness and eternity, decorates himself with this sign, which represents a palm rib. He is represented kneeling, with arms raised, as a sky bearer. Heh carries in himself, in his aspect as god of the wind, characteristics of both Shu and Amun. His image, with palm ribs on his head, also indicates the number "million" (cf. p. 73).

1.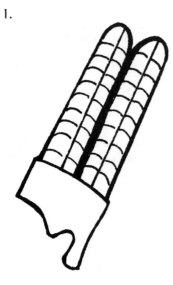

2.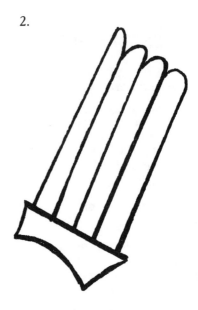

3.

4.

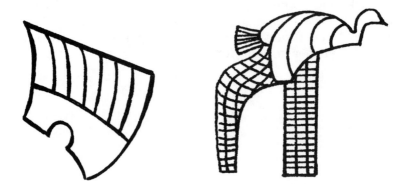

Head coverings of the gods
Amun, Anhur, Anukis, and Nekhebet/Mut

HEAD COVERINGS OF THE GODS, I

The head coverings of the gods are identifying characteristics and symbolize the scope of their power or their membership. As hieroglyphics, they indicate either the field of influence of the deity or a personification thereof. If a god is represented in an embodiment, he usually receives human form and wears his typical head ornament. Here, however, the time sequence must also be observed, since the Egyptian gods often changed their fields of influence and their signs over time. Such changes were mainly based on political influences, such as, for example, the unification of Upper and Lower Egypt. To specify the deities on wall paintings, therefore, other attributes of their power are considered, including scepters, symbols, clothing, and similar things.

1. The double-feather crown identifies the creator god, Amun, who later was worshiped as the sun god, Amun-Re. In this way, a connection was created with the sky and sun god, Horus, who likewise wore this as a head ornament.

2. The four-feather crown stands for Anhur.

3. Anukis, who was viewed as the lady of the sky and the Nile water, decorated herself with this feather ornament. She was represented as either a human or as a gazelle, which was to embody her grace and speed.

4. The vulture headdress is both the head covering of the vulture goddess Nekhebet, the land goddess of Upper Egypt, and also the original goddess Mut, who was viewed as the wife of Amun. In rare cases, Isis also appears with this head ornament, when she is represented as in mourning.

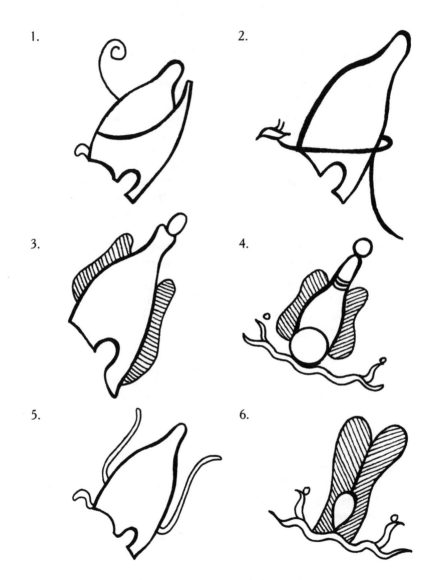

1.

2.

3.

4.

5.

6.

Head coverings of the gods
Atum/Horus, Osiris, Satis, Reshef, Khnemu, and Sebek

HEAD COVERINGS OF THE GODS, II

1. The double crown represents the creator god, Atum. The god Horus also wears this head ornament in his function as ruler over Upper and Lower Egypt. The combined crown symbolizes the unification of the land.

2. The Atef crown decorated the head of Osiris.

3. Satis, the source of water and wife of the creator god Khnemu, wears this Upper Egyptian crown, which is decorated with two antelope horns. Since Khnemu is often equated with Re, Satis is also called the "eye of Re."

4. The Upper Egyptian crown of Reshef bears a gazelle head. Originally, this god of Canaan was considered to be a bringer of plagues. Only later was he was worshiped as a war god. He appears in human form with the crown shown here, as well as with a shield and club, which served as attributes of his power.

5. The crown of the god Khnemu shows stylized ram's horns, since he was also often represented with a ram's head. In him, as creator god, the gods of the sky (Re), earth (Geb), air (Shu), and the underworld (Osiris) were united.

6. The crocodile god Sebek wears this crown. The line of waves shows the water of the Nile, which arose from his sweat.

SACRED SIGNS

1.

2.

3.

THE CONCEPT OF "GOD" IN GENERAL

1. Since the 5th Dynasty, the verbal sign for "god" was written in this form, which shows a sitting deity in human form. The squatting form is covered here in a body cloth, which covers the whole body. The ceremonial beard has the typical curve, which identifies the figure as a deity. Originally, this beard was a typical identification of the god Osiris, and the meaning of the hieroglyphic was supposedly expanded to other deities with the growth of his cult.

2. The picture of the god standard, which bears a hawk, represents an early form of the hieroglyphic described above. By approximately about 4000 B.C., at the beginning of the distinctive animal cult, this sign was entered in documents. In the various Egyptian provinces there were so many hawk-shaped deities that the hawk became a general concept of "god."

3. This universal symbol for "god" probably developed from the pre-dynastic time. The object that is represented in this way is still problematic today. From some clearer representations, it can be concluded that this involves a fetish bound with strips of material, where a loose strip of cloth fluttered in the wind like a waving flag. This raised flag then showed the presence of a god at a particular place.

1.

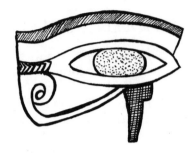

2.

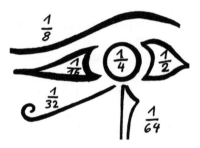

3.   4.

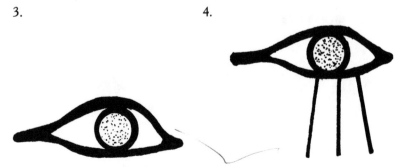

Horus eyes (utchats)

THE HORUS EYE

1. The sun and the moon were the eyes of the god Horus. The Horus eye was a very popular amulet in Egypt, since it embodied the eternally returning restoration of universal harmony. According to myth, the envious god Set had once torn the eye from his nephew Horus after he had killed and dismembered his father, Osiris. The moon god, Thoth, however, restored the eye and healed it. Horus the brought it to his father, Osiris, in order for him to give it new life. Since then, the Horus eye (utchat) was considered to be the prototype of the sacrifice ceremony. Therefore, it was found in portrayals of the lotus god, Nefertem.

The left eye of Horus stood for the moon and the past. It received feminine forces, while the right eye embodied the active, creative, and masculine forces of the sun and the future. The two eyes thus guaranteed the power of omniscience. As the most important protective amulet, it promised eternal life.

2. The individual parts of the moon eye, which Set has ripped out, were assigned values as fractions. The numbers totaled 63/64, since Set allowed the 64th part of the Utchat eye to be lost.

3. The eye as a hieroglyphic (sound value "irt") relates directly to the seeing organ and the ability to see. The magical force that emanates from the eye is also represented in this way. In general, a fire element was assigned to the eye, since it can receive light and colors. When the god Horus opened his eyes, the light that brightens the universe emanated from it; if he closed them, then darkness returned.

4. The sign for the weeping eye stood for "mi," to weep. It also relates to the old creation myth, according to which are supposed to have originated from the tears of the highest god, the sun.

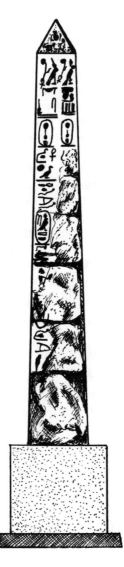

Obelisk

SUN TEMPLE

In Heliopolis, a monolithic stone was worshipped for the first time, which was viewed as the first manifestation of the original god, Amun-Cheops, since the rays coming out of the sun were to strike it first. It was called Benben. In the Fifth Dynasty, obelisks were already found in all sun temples. Two of them were used in each of the temple courts of the New Kingdom to establish and expand their importance in the sun-moon cycle, whereby one of them embodied the sun of the day and the other the sun of the night. The offerings brought to the stone temples also resemble the shape of an obelisk.

The shape and the original meaning of the stone monuments have still not been completely clarified today. In general, the obelisk symbolized the original hill, from which the creator god arose. Whether this involves a petrified sun ray or a phallic sign can not be stated with certainty. Since, however, the significance of sexual potency and creative power as a revelation of life energy was predominant in the religious awareness of the Egyptians, the obelisk is rather to be viewed as a fertility symbol of the creative power of the sun god.

1.

2.

Sun symbols

SYMBOLS OF THE SUN

1. Even in ancient times, the sky was represented by two out-spread wings. With the addition of the sun disk in the Fifth Dynasty, the sign became a sun symbol. The winged sun involves a symbol of royal protection, recognizable from the two uraeus snakes coiled around the sun disk, which, in some New Kingdom forms also wear the crowns of Upper and Lower Egypt.

2. This ornament from the grave of Tutankhamen shows the winged Khepera, the symbol of the morning sun. It embodies the original god, who created himself by coming forth without creation from the underworld and rose from the womb of his mother, Nut, to the eastern sky. Khepera was considered to be a manifestation of Atum and Re. This beetle-shaped god also played an important role in the belief in the resurrection.

Star as the soul of the deceased

STAR

The shape of the hieroglyphic goes back to the starfish, which is found in the Red Sea. The Egyptians equated the stars of the night sky with the original sea. Therefore, they connected the starfish with the stars, which are almost always represented in yellow or red colors. The written sign for the stars also denoted the teacher, whose task of teaching was compared to the dangerous task of navigating by heavenly bodies. Especially in ancient times, the stars were interpreted as the souls of the deceased, and they are therefore seen very frequently in paintings on sarcophagi.

According to the myth, countless soul stars followed the sun on its travels through the kingdoms of light and darkness. The deities also had their embodiments in the stars. Thus Isis was seen as Sirius, who followed the soul of Osiris in the form of Orion.

In later times, the sky was divided into 36 regions, each presided over by a star or constellation. These so-called gods of the sky each ruled over a time period of ten days. The circumpolar stars were viewed with the highest respect, since in contrast to all other heavenly bodies, they did not set in the west.

Naos

SHRINE

The shrines of the gods each contained a statue of the deity worshiped in the temple. They were mostly made of wood, since they were carried on the barques of the gods in processions, but stone and precious metals were also used.

The drawing shows the typical form of the shrine called naos, with the roof curved to the front, which was borrowed from the temple of Upper Egypt. Almost all shrines were richly decorated with hieroglyphics and pictorial representations. The height of a naos seldom exceeded the height of a person, except for the naos of Mendes, which was seven meters high and four meters wide.

The shrine that contained the deity stood, as a rule, in the rearmost corner of a chamber of the temple, which was accessible to only a few priests. The plinth (base) often shows representations of kings carrying the sky, since the naos embodied the space of the sky. If the shrine was opened, then symbolically the entrances to the sky were opened to the field of power held by the deity as represented by the statue.

Barque with naos

BARQUE WITH SHRINE OF GODS

To make the existence and presence of the gods known to people, processions were held at regular intervals, in which statues of the gods were carried along. The most sacred image of the deity in such parades remained, however, concealed in the closed naos (shrine), which was located on the sacred barque. The basic form of the barque imitated that of a Nile boat, decorated at its bow and stern with the head of the god or his sacred animal.

During the procession, the barques were carried by the deity's priests on their shoulders. Other sacred barques were suitable as boats for transporting the shrine on water. The route of such a procession was determined most precisely before the start, and on the way they stopped many times to announce the oracle, which had been asked in advance. Most of the time, other deities that were worshipped in other cities were permitted to visit, so that they could communicate with one another.

The barque was based on the myth of the sun god in the sacred regions. It was said that he never left it while travelling across the sky throughout the day and at night he had it pulled by jackals over the sand of the underworld. Other, earthly gods used a barque only when they visited each other or participated in processions.

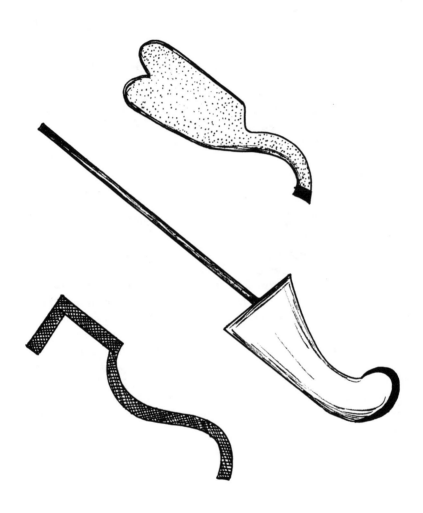

Devices for the ritual of opening the mouth

MAGICAL ANIMATION: THE RITUAL OF OPENING THE MOUTH

The drawing shows the three most important devices that were used during the ritual of opening the mouth. The ritual was performed whenever a statue or even the mummy of a deceased person was to be animated magically. This was to enable the deceased to make further use of his organs.

For statues, the animation magic was performed in the gold house, whereas mummies stayed in the embalming room. After the mummy or the image had been cleaned as prescribed, a front quarter of freshly slaughtered beef was sacrificed, which means it was presented as food. The animal sacrifice was to give bodily strength to the object being animated. Then the face of the statue or mummy was touched with the devices pictured here. In this way, it was given the energy and elements that were vital to it. Finally, it was dressed, anointed, and taken to the sacrifice meal.

From the viewpoint of magic, therefore, it is not surprising that there were repeated reports of curses and unexplainable events in connection with the excavations in Egypt, for the magical animation that was practiced in several cultures was quite capable of creating artificial beings that could act in the psychic and physical worlds for unlimited periods of time.

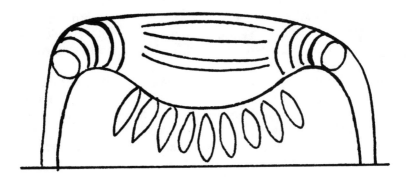

Gold

METAL OF THE GODS: GOLD

The sign and also the hieroglyphic for gold can be seen here (see page 73). From ancient times, gold was considered to be the metal of the gods, especially of the sun god. Thus the sun god, Re, was called the "gold mountain that illuminates the earth." In the Egyptians' concept, the limbs of the gods were made of pure gold, and the metal itself could confer godly abilities. For this reason, the Egyptians devoted incredible amounts of labor and time to obtain the precious metal and did not fear accidents and dangerous expeditions.

A golden face mask was placed on deceased princely persons, whereas simple people had to be satisfied with yellow paint. The graves of pharaohs, which were lavishly decorated with God, were called the "house of gold." In the time of the New Kingdom, the goddesses Isis and Nephthys were represented as kneeling on the sign for gold. In this way, people attempted to assure their protection.

Sphinx

SYMBOL OF KINGSHIP: THE SPHINX

The shape of the sphinx developed from the age-old identification of the king with a lion, where the head of the animal was replaced by the head of the ruler. Originally, sphinxes were placed at the entrances to temples as symbols of royal power. In the New Kingdom, however, the sphinx was assigned only the position of watcher over graves and temples. It can be seen in this way also in the best-known sphinx of King Khephren at Giza. In the New Kingdom, the sphinx was then placed in a relationship with the sun god, Amun-Re, and received a ram's head instead of a human head. Another, typical characteristic of this mythical being is the royal headcloth that covered the neck and was replaced by a lion's mane only on the Middle Kingdom sphinx at Tanis.

It can be said in summary that the sphinx represented an embodiment of the earthly and divine characteristics of the pharaoh.

Note: the Egyptian concept of the sphinx is not comparable to the Greek sphinx, which exists in their language as a female being.

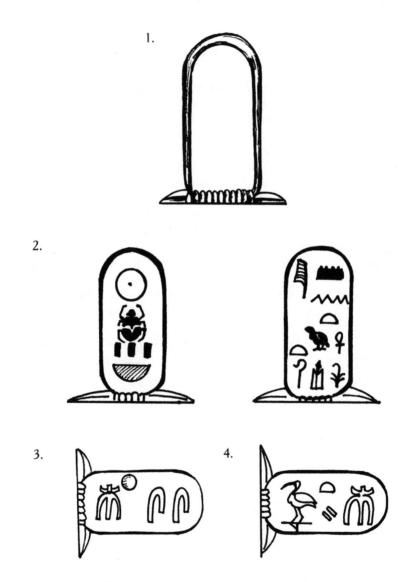

Royal ring and royal cartouches

THE ROYAL CARTOUCHE

1. The royal ring, which was made from a knotted rope, symbolized the cosmos, "that which encircles the sun." The oval shape of the cartouche developed from the circular royal ring. It was better suited to accept numerous written signs. As magic amulets, cartouches had the task of protecting the king. The sarcophagi of some rulers were given the shape of the royal ring, in order to give expression to the world-dominating power of the pharaoh.

2. These two drawings are name cartouches of Tutankhamen; the left one contains his birth name. This can be recognized by the sun symbol, which designates him as the son of Re. The right cartouche shows his royal name.

3. This cartouch of King Ramses consists of signs that have phonetic values, with which his name was written.

4. This sign has been identified as the royal ring of the pharaoh Thutmosis. The inscription contains the hieroglyphic of the ibis-headed god, Thoth, and the birth sign on the right side, which is translated "given to the world by Thoth."

The ways in which royal names were written in cartouches generally varied a great deal, since they could be read either in their phonetic sound values or as symbolic pictorial representations (see page 33).

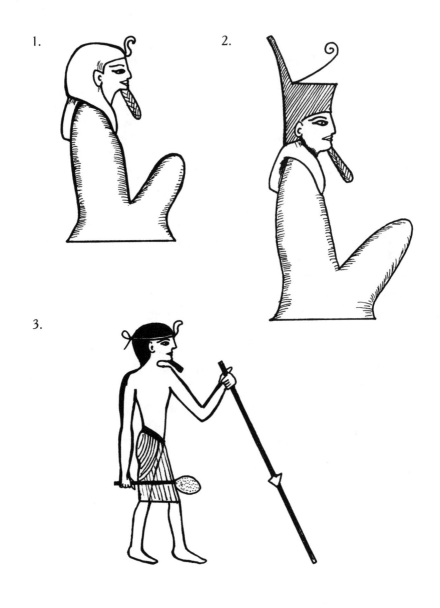

1.

2.

3.

THE KING IN WRITING

1. This hieroglyphic was used when the words of the pharaoh were written in the first person. The god-like status of the king is also clear in this sign, which is very similar to the symbol for "god" (see page 137). To differentiate it, the figure is provided with a wig and a straight beard. The royal uraeus snake is added as another attribute.

2. A variant of the sign, from the period before the unification of the two kingdoms, shows the hieroglyphic for the king with the crown of Lower Egypt. It designates the Lower Egyptian ruler. For the pharaoh of Upper Egypt, the hieroglyphic was provided with the white crown of Upper Egypt (not shown here).

3. This hieroglyphic, which shows the active ruler with staff and scepter, was likewise used in writing and on wall paintings.

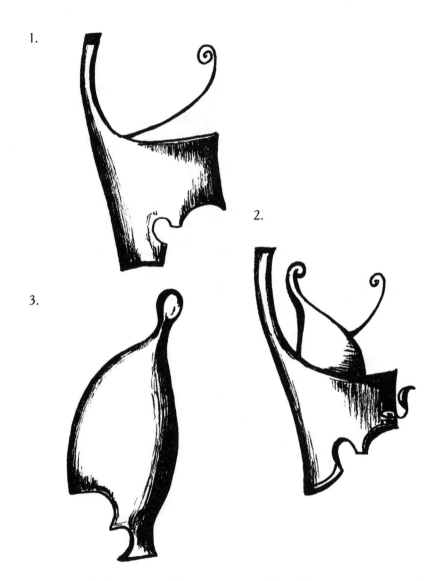

Red crown, white crown, and double crown

CROWNS OF THE PHARAOHS

1. This picture shows the "red crown" of Lower Egypt. It was considered to be the embodiment of the Lower Egyptian protective god, Buto, who was represented in the form of a snake.

2. The "white crown" of Upper Egypt was the symbol of the royal land god, Nekhebet, the vulture goddess.

3. Here, the double crown can be seen, which unites the two forms described above. It was worn by the pharaohs after the merger of the two kingdoms about 2850 BC by the legendary King Menes. From then on, the uraeus snake also decorated the front of the crown as a protective flame.

In general, the crowns expressed the power of their bearers, who were often viewed as persons authorized by the gods. They also showed the characteristics of a ruler. Thus, after the 18th Dynasty, they wore a tight-fitting blue helmet with golden decorations similar to a war helmet.

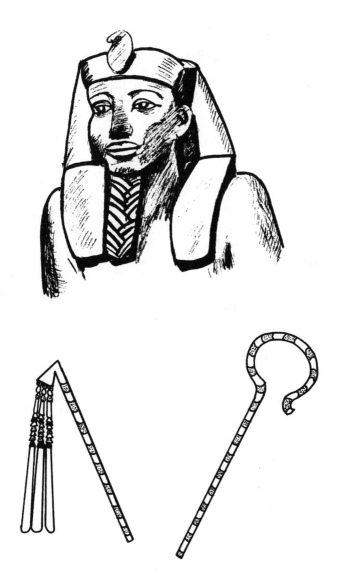

Insignia of royal power

ROYAL HEADCLOTH

The royal headcloth was the symbol of the Upper Egyptian vulture goddess Nekhebet, who traditionally accompanied him into battle and protected him there with a white cloth.

The artificial beard, braided like a pigtail, was considered to be a sign of dignity, both for gods and kings. Since blue hair was attributed to deities, their beards also bore the color of lapis lazuli.

CROOK AND FLAIL

The most important royal insignia can be seen in this drawing: the crook and the flail. The crook originally developed from the shepherd's staff and was used to hold unruly animals by the leg. In this long variant, it can also be seen as an attribute of the shepherd god, Anezti. In various other implementations, it was borne as a scepter by higher dignitaries. In hieroglyphic writing, the symbol of the crook stands for the concept "to rule."

The flail was always assigned to the gods Osiris and Min. In the hand of the king, it was a symbol of rulership. It was interpreted either as a fly whisk or as the shepherd's whip of the god Anezti, who originated in the eastern region. Since fly whisks were popularly used in the African area to drive evil beings away, this meaning is more probable from the overall African connection.

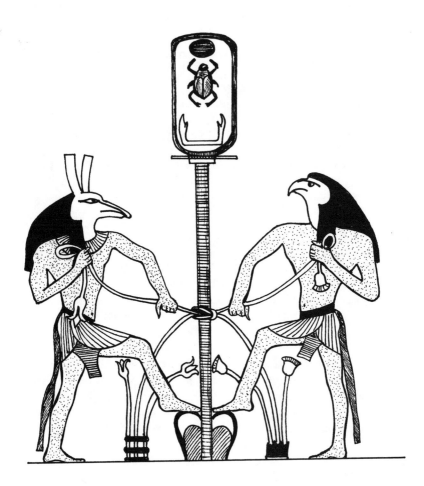

Set and Horus join the heraldic plants of Upper and Lower

UNIFICATION OF UPPER AND LOWER EGYPT

The historical unification of Upper and Lower Egypt was often symbolized by the combination of the adversaries Horus and Set. They are standing around the heraldic plants of the two lands, the lily (Upper Egypt) and papyrus (Lower Egypt), from which the symbol for the lungs arises from an air tube. This representation is surmounted by a representation of the name cartouche of the current king.

Pictures of this kind were placed on statues of the ruler at the site of the throne, because with every transfer of office the symbolic act of unification of the two lands was reenacted. In variants, the god Thoth can also appear instead of Set.

Another representation of the historical events shows the unification of female forces as the combination of the two protective goddesses Buto and Nekhebet in their forms as cobra and vulture.

1.

2.

3.

4.

Ankh, loop of life, tet, and shen

LIFE SIGNS

1. Since ancient Egyptian times, the ankh has been the symbol of eternal life, in this world and in the otherworld. It is connected with tradition in modern times in that it was adopted as the cross of the Coptic Christians in Egypt.

In many representations, the gods are holding an ankh in their hand or extending it to people. This involves the breath of life made visible, to some extent the divine spark, through which life can first come into being. It further embodies the life-giving characteristics of the elements air and water. The origin of its shape has not yet been clarified. It may involve a magical knot, in which case sexual relationships probably also played a role. Another interpretation sees it as a combination of the T-shaped Osiris cross, and the oval of Isis as the key that locks away the secrets of life.

2. The loop of life was often worn by the people in this form as a knot amulet. Like the ankh, it stands for unchangeability and immortality.

3. The tet sign, which is also called the "blood of Isis," was mostly given to the dead as an amulet. It resembles an ankh whose arms are hanging down. In combination with the tet pillar on temple wails and sarcophagi, it indicates the unification of opposite forces and thereby the eternally renewing life force.

4. Here, the shen ring and at the same time the hieroglyphic for "eternity" can be seen. In wall paintings, it is often worn by divine animals, such as the hawk, for example. People also liked to wear the sign of the eternal cycle as an amulet for protection against diseases and disaster.

1.

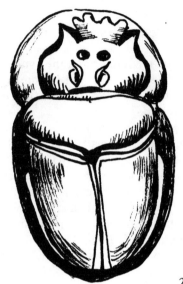

2.

Scarab

Ⱥ Ⱥ Ⱥ Ⱥ Ⱥ Ⱥ Ⱥ Ⱥ Ⱥ Ⱥ Ⱥ Ⱥ Ⱥ Ⱥ Ⱥ

THE SYMBOL OF RENEWAL OF LIFE: SCARAB

1. The dung beetle can be an amulet. The Egyptians saw in the dung ball, which these beetles tirelessly roll before them, the image of the sun disk and a manifestation of Khepera, the god of the rising sun. They also assumed that only male animals exist in this species, since its descendants come forth from a dung heap after a while, as if by a miracle and without conception. It therefore became a symbol of the master world-builder, who was formed from himself. The scarab was also considered to be an aspect of the god of creation, Atum, and the sun god. Its powerful amulet was buried with the deceased as a symbol of new life and placed in the position of the heart.

2. When the traditional inscription of the underside of the scarab amulet is translated, it reads: "May your name be preserved, may children come to you."

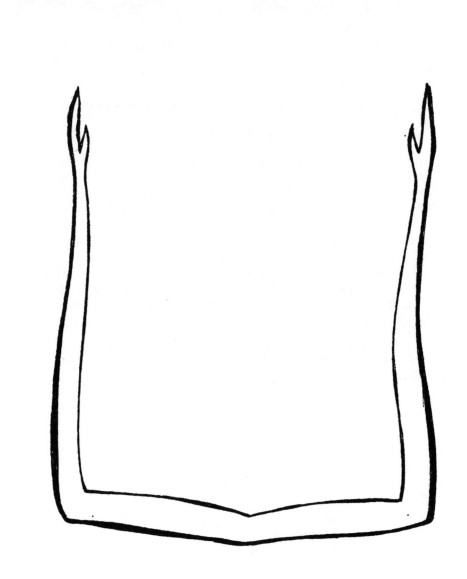

Ka

THE SYMBOL OF THE IMMORTAL SPIRIT: KA

The mental/spiritual life power of living beings was called ka and symbolized by two raised arms. By this defensive position, the talisman was to be able to keep negative powers away that could threaten vital energy. The ka head ornament was often worn by the pharaohs, since, in addition to its protective function, it also symbolized the spiritual power of the gods, which could be transferred to the king.

In the oldest times, ka was a name for the male reproductive ability and was handed down from father to son. It was thus not only the carrier of the life force of an individual, but also a watcher over inheritances. Very soon, however, its significance was extended to the entire mental and spiritual power of the one who wore it, and it became a symbol of the fine-matter body, which is born with the physical body and lives on after its death. Thus the concept "to die" is also written with the words "to go to his ka." Since the ka also needed nourishment, offerings for it were either added to the grave or represented on wall paintings, which was fully sufficient as spiritual food for the spirit. Food was considered, in addition to its function of maintaining the body, also as the carrier of the spiritual life forces.

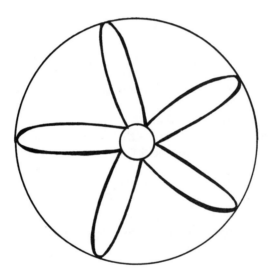

Cycle of rebirth and the underworld

THE OTHERWORLD

The circle that surrounds the star here symbolizes the cycle of eternal rebirth on the one hand and the closed region of the underworld on the other, where all the dead that had passed their acceptance test resided.

Burial ceremonies and spiritual leaders on the other side were supposed to make it easier for souls on the other side to move about securely. In this otherworld, there was a strict separation between sinners and good souls, who were each assigned to their own regions. Righteous people could therefore expect a state of paradise. However, all souls on the other side had to accomplish certain works that were useful to their personal development.

Shadow body

THE SHADOW

This wall painting shows the shadow of the deceased Nakhtamun, as he is leaving his temple-shaped tomb. The shadow is viewed as the fine-matter body of the dead person, which can leave the grave at any time, accompanied by the soul bird, Ba. In living people, the physical body is connected with the life force, ka, the soul-spirit, ba, and the shadow in a unit. Therefore, one can therefore describe the shadow as the astral body, which lives on after death, mostly unseen by the living.

In general, the concept of the shadow in the hot desert country is also assigned a protective function. So the "shadow of Re," fell upon the king, who, of course, stood in the favor of the sun god.

Sarcophagus

THE HOUSE OF THE DEAD: THE SARCOPHAGUS

The wooden sarcophagus depicted contained the mummy of a priest of Thebes. It served to protect the remains and was understood as the house of the dead. Painted doors on the inner and outer walls were to make it possible for the dead person to leave the coffin. Also, painted eyes on the inside of the coffin, which were seen frequently in the New Period, were to make contact with the outside world.

The coffin was decorated with many magical sayings and pictorial representations, which were to guide the powers of eternity to the dead person. Thus we recognize, for example, Nephthys and Isis, who wafted the breath of life to the dead with their wings. The four Horus suns represent the internal organs, which were stored separately in canopic jars. The image of the sky god, Nut, was often applied to the lid of the coffin, as a sign of the resurrection. A picture of a vulture is often found on the breast part of coffins, in order to protect the heart of the deceased. In the New Period, however, the sacred scarab appeared in its place.

In addition, the coffins were generally provided with the symbols of the individual protective deities, and the names and rank of the dead person can be read on intersecting strips of writing.

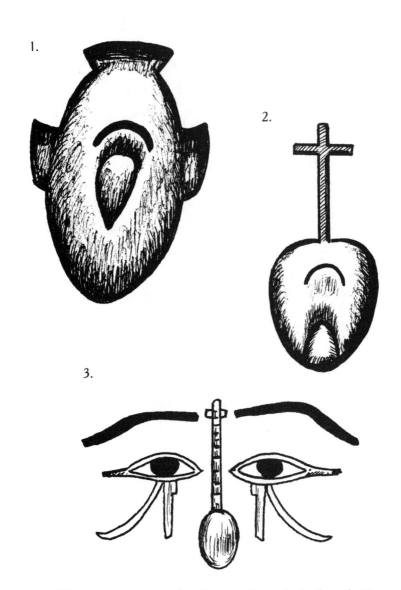

1.

2.

3.

Heart, heart with air tubes, and symbol of perfection

SEAT OF THE PERSONALITY: THE HEART

1. This sign is a natural reproduction of a sheep's heart. As the central organ, the heart was made responsible for all processes in the body, spirit, and soul. Since it pumps the blood to all parts of the body, it was viewed as the seat of the personality.

In ancient Egypt, there was already a completely correct understanding of the anatomical connections of the circulation and the search for rational/scientific explanations. In addition, the religious concept, according to which all emotional and intellectual processes started from the heart, had equal status.

Because of the central role of this organ, it was also the only one that was left in the body during mummification, since only in this way could the dead person live on. In order that the heart could not testify against the deceased when it was weighed against a feather in the otherworld, a wrapped heart scarab was buried with the dead person as an amulet.

2. This hieroglyphic, with the meaning "good," which represents a heart with air tubes, often identifies good and honest people, whose mouth always spoke the truth. At that time, saying what the heart thought was considered to be the highest virtue.

This symbol also stood for truth, which was also based on the understanding about the heart.

3. Many pictorial representations also combine this symbol for "perfection," as in this picture of a wife of the god Amun. In this connection, it was also considered to be a sign that brought good luck.

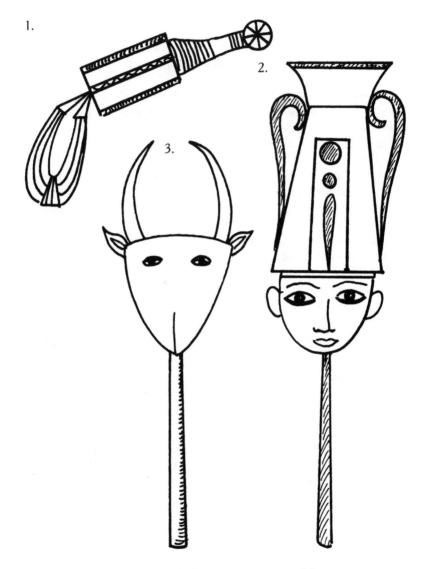

Menat pearl chain, sistrum, and bat

MAGICAL OBJECTS: MENAT CHAIN, SISTRUM, AND BAT

1. The Menat pearl chain was considered to be an ornament of the goddess Hathor, with healing powers. It consisted of a heavy chain, whose weight was held balanced by a counterpoise that represented a stylized female fertility puppet. Menat chains were also worn by other goddesses, although only in connection with the Hathor cult. The priestesses of Hathor also used this ornament together with the sistrum to make noise during ceremonies. For this, they grasped the chain with one hand and moved it rhythmically up and down, whereby the metal parts that were included generated a typical rattle.

2. The sistrum was the rattle instrument with which the goddess Hathor granted her blessings. Its sound was compared with the noise of the papyrus thicket, and it was therefore attributed with the power to invoke the deities. The female aspects of the bird-of-prey goddesses, which were especially dangerous, could be pacified by the sistrum. This instrument was generally made of metal and showed the double face of the goddess, one of which embodied the Isis aspect and the other that of Naphthys. In the Egyptian dualism, these two goddesses stood for life and death. The goddess bears on her head a sacred shrine, framed by its cow horns.

3. The bat represents an older variant of the sistrum and shows the cow-headed goddess Bat. Over time, this form of the rattle instrument blended with the symbolism of the goddess Hathor into the two-faced form of the sistrum, where one face looked forward and the other backward.

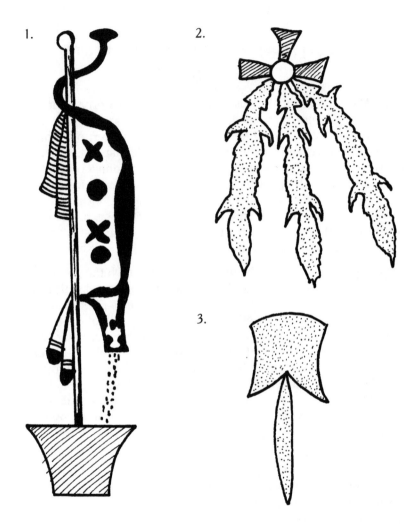

*Cowhide fetish Imiut, symbolic sign for birth, cowhide
hieroglyphic*

THE IMIUT FETISH

1. The story of this fetish goes back to the First Dynasty. A headless cow hide is attached to a pole standing in a pot. Its task consisted of protecting the royal throne. Only later did the Imiut become interwoven with the cult of the god of the dead, Anubis, and thereafter, as a wooden replica, it was buried with noble deceased persons.

ANIMAL SKINS

2. Animal skins often characterize the transition from one world to the next. Because of this, the symbolic sign for birth consists of three knotted fox skins, which were to manifest body, spirit, and soul in this world.

3. The hieroglyphic for cowhide can be seen in Figure 3. In texts, it could also denote leather goods or the skins of other animals. The skin was generally seed as the medium for outer transformation, which also permitted an internal transformation.

1.

2.

Tet pillars

FETISH OF OSIRIS AND PTAH: TET

1. Originally, the cult of the tet pillar came from prehistoric time, and its significance at that time has still not been fully clarified today. It is certain that from the beginning it involved a fertility symbol. As a hieroglyphic, it derives from this the sound value "ddi," which means "duration" and "permanence."

This fetish consisted either of a post, to which supported grain sheaves are attached, or else it involved a tree with branches that have been trimmed and bound together. In general, the tet played an important role in the fertility rites of the land. It was the symbol of power, through which the power of the grain was to be preserved. In Memphis, very early on, there was already a tet priest, who at that time was equated with the local chief god, Ptah. There arose the custom of "erecting the tet." At the same time, the triumphal resurrection of the necropolis god Sokaris was celebrated with this ritual, who was in turn brought into connection with Ptah. The ritual ceremony was performed by the king himself, assisted by the priests, and was associated with hope for an enduring, stable kingdom.

As an amulet, the tet pillar was to generate stability and immortal power.

2. The second variant shows Osiris as a tet, symbol of victory over his brother and enemy, Set. With Osiris, the pillar was brought into connection for the first time in the New Kingdom with the god of the dead, Sokaris. Since the tet symbolized the backbone of the god, it was often painted on the bottom of coffins, at the place where the spine of the dead person was placed.

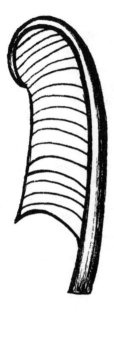

Feathers and feather fans

FEATHERS AND FANS

The hieroglyphic for "feather" can also have the phonetic value "mzct," and thereby the meaning truth and justice. In its form, the hieroglyphic corresponds to a white ostrich feather, which was generally assigned to lightness and weightlessness and thus also symbolized the element air. It is also the sign for the goddess Maat, who regulated the cosmic balance and the relationships between gods and humans. Maintaining reasonable cosmic harmony was then considered the highest obligation of the king, who had to implement the divine rules in practice in his kingdom. This symbol is also found often in grave inscriptions in connection with the god Anubis, who holds a balance. On one side there is the heart of the dead person and on the other side, a feather. In this case, the feather is equated with the lightness of a pure heart and with truth.

The lower illustration shows a servant with the feather fan, who is bringing ointment. Fans were considered to be transmitters of divine protection and were assigned as the cult symbols of the fertility goddess, Min. In paintings, they are often seen behind sacred animals. As providers of shade, fans were also brought into connection with the shadows of people. This meaning applies primarily to representations combined with the ba bird.

GESTURES AND ACTIONS

Attitude of humility

WORSHIP

This attitude of worship is also exhibitedin the hieroglyphic with which this action is described. In this case, the praying person can have either a standing or a sitting posture. Especially typical is the gesture of humility, holding the hands open in the direction of the deity. A representation of the god is often missing in the pictures, but his invisible presence is indicated by the attitude of the praying person. Traditional representations often show the pharaoh, as he holds his palms toward a deity in the gesture of humility.

Foreign rulers or prisoners can often be seen in this attitude of humility before the pharaoh, in order to confirm their capitulation and give expression to their defenselessness.

Gesture of pleading

REQUESTOR

A priest is bowing here, during a procession, in the typical gesture of a requestor before a deity. Those who bore the sacred barque that contained the divine image were also obligated to raise their free arm and hold the palm upward.

An important characteristic of the body language was the slight bend of the back, which was to make it clear that the person concerned bears no kind of aggressiveness.

This hieroglyphic, which stands for the word "call/ask," describes the same pose as the man shown here demonstrates. Here, one arm is always shown hanging down, while the other is held up, more or less at an angle, and the palm is directed upward or to the front.

1.

2.

Hatshepsut and Thutmosis III

ROYAL HUMILITY

1. This relief shows Queen Hatshepsut, depicted here in human form, in a kneeling attitude before the god Amun. Pharaohs are generally portrayed in such a humble attitude only in connection with deities. The sitting god Amun is raising his hand here in a blessing over the head of Hatshepsut.

2. Thutmosis III is also represented here kneeling humbly before Amun (not visible in the picture). He is holding in his hands two offering cups with gifts he is presenting to the god. Thutmosis is performing the traditional gesture of offering here.

Powerlessness of the enemy

PRISONER

The written sign that shows a man in this defenseless position stands for the concept of "enemy" or "rebellion."

In Egypt, representations of the enemy in such a powerless, immobile attitude served for magical defense. It was believed that events that were manifested pictorially also had to have their effects on the real level. Representations of prisoners in images and reliefs always show the typical facial features of the peoples to whom they belong. On an execution stake, they awaited certain death. In the old period, prisoners of war were still offered to the gods.

Clay figures in the form of bound enemies served as magical wishes. They resembled an enemy ruler and bore his name. As is common in other voodoo cultures, these images were then ritually beaten in order to destroy the person.

Greeting the sun god

JUBILATION

In general, this picture of a male figure who is striking his chest with one fist and holding the other fist above his head express his joy.

This probably really involves motions in which the man or the god beats his chest alternately with both fists. In the sky of the gods, the arrival of the sun god is celebrated in this manner. On earth, the pharaoh was greeted by his court in exactly the same way. His followers accompanied the singing of hymns by drumming on their chests powerfully. In a magical way, the feeling of unity and the power of the king were strengthened. When this ceremonial gesture was performed, a half-kneeling attitude was assumed, in which one foot was kept flat.

In rare cases, the hieroglyphic corresponding to this picture could also stand in connection with a lamentation for the dead.

In this drawing, a jackal-headed deity can be seen, who is greeting the sun god ecstatically.

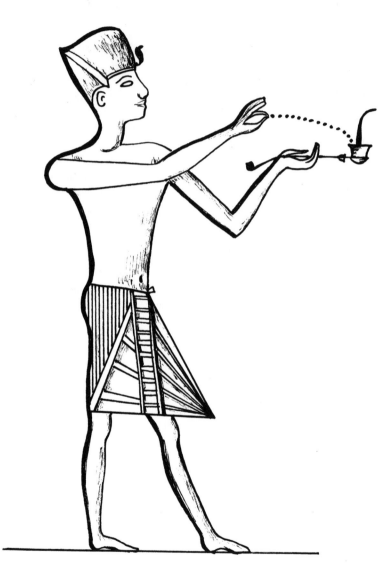

Incense for purification

THE ACTION OF INCENSE

In this frieze, Thutmosis III is presenting incense on the occasion of a barque procession received by Queen Hatshepsut. The sacred smoke was considered to be a supernatural celestial fragrance that was able to drive demonic powers away. In ceremonies, it served to purify the sites where they took place. In this way, for example, men could be assured when an oracle was questioned, that the answers really can from the gods.

Because of its good smell, the sacred smoke was also used in higher society to make the room air aromatic.

As a hieroglyphic, the incense process was reduced to the representation of the incense vessel depicted here.

Priest during ritual washing

PURITY

Internal and external purity was generally considered to be the highest virtue. For this reason, the priests observed a whole series of religious taboos and attempted to become respected by the gods with whom they associated through various ascetic abilities. This included the shaving of the head and body of the servants of the gods and abstaining from fish. Their clothing generally consisted of linen, since this material did not derive from a living being.

The drawing shows the priest Niaii during ritual washing, which he is receiving from the sacred vessel of the gods. In old Egypt, people knew that the magnetic power of water could free one from all external and internal impurities. For this reason, the priests washed themselves several times a day.

The written picture for the word "pure" likewise sketches a man in the attitude of offering, who is receiving the sacred flood.

1.

2.

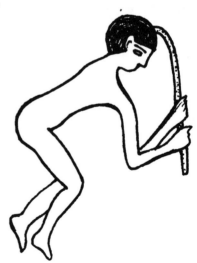

Symbols of death

THE ATTITUDE OF DYING

1. The form of a dying man has twisted limbs. The representation of a violent death was frightening and unnatural for the Egyptians. Therefore, representations of this kind always relate to foreign, enemy peoples and are found in scenes of either war or hunting. Death was viewed as a painful reversal of life, and efforts were continually made to prevent this moment by means of various magical means. The constant efforts concerning life after death and the eternal return also contributed to the exclusion of this feared segment from consciousness.

2. This hieroglyphic for the words "to die" and "enemy" is the only one that symbolizes the moment of death. In later periods, it also served to describe suicide. The attitude of the falling man with blood flowing from his head provides a certain dynamic. After the 20th Dynasty, the blood was often replaced by an axe; this was more reminiscent of suicide.

Victor's pose

TRIUMPH

The written sign corresponding to this picture has the meaning of "to be high," or "to rejoice."

General Horemheb is in the pose of a victor in this drawing. Raising the arms was in Old Egypt, just as today, a gesture of extreme joy and triumph. The feeling of lightness is given expression, in that the arms of the person concerned are always lifted above the head, which represents the connection with heaven. Actions of this kind are often found in pictures in which an oracle announces good news or a court decision in this world or the next in favor of the defendant. Also, subjects who received a special honor from the pharaoh and military commanders who had won a battle broke out into this kind of jubilation.

Victory of the king over the powers of darkness

SUBJECTION

This picture shows the king Thutmosis IV striking an Asian in battle. The defeated person can be easily identified as a foreigner by his hairstyle. By pulling a lock of hair, the pharaoh is demonstrating his unlimited power over his opponent. This traditional pose of "striking the enemy," symbolized the victory of the king over the chaotic powers of darkness.

In an extended sense, this action also relates to the separation of the sacred from the profane, since the military scenes represented often have nothing to do with the real world. This meaning of the club or the rod with which the king is preparing to strike has not yet been clarified. It probably involves rather a symbolic, magical weapon for driving off the negative influences of evil spirits than a real military device.

Strength, concentration, goal awareness

PURPOSEFULNESS

The bow has always symbolized the power of the king over subject peoples, and it was assigned to the goddess of war, Neith.
Therefore, the archer also came to epitomize the soldier. The
powers of concentration, speed, and goal awareness were associated with him. Since archers mainly involved African merce-
naries or members of Nubian tribes, they were usually represented with dark skin. Their clothing consisted of a leather gir-
dle, which did not restrict their freedom of movement. They
wore a band around their head with a feather as a sign of the
state of war.

The hieroglyphic of the archer, which denotes the "army,"
shows the warrior either in a tense, seated position or in a
proud, striding pose.

HISTORICAL
PERSONALITIES

The reformer and visionary

AKHENATON

The revolutionary personality Akhenaton is the most disputed one in the history of Old Egypt. In documents of the 19th Dynasty, he is even called the "criminal of Amarna," while in later times he is often titled "bold spirit" and "earnest idealist." His birth name was Akhenaton, which was known as until his 5th regnal year, was Amenhotep IV. Before he took office as the successor to his father, Amenhotep III, he was married to Nefertiti. He was a great mystic, and he was far ahead of the consciousness of his time. Since he encountered rejection among his people with his revolutionary ideas, he attempted to implement the concept of his world view by force. He was the first historical leader to introduce a monotheistic religion, that is, he fought against the worship of the old gods and elevated Aton as the only god. For this purpose, he had the names of the gods carved out of the older pictures and sculptures, in order to take away their identity. The new god of the kingdom, Aton, was then not worshiped in an intimate human or animal form, but in a stylized form as a sun disk, whose rays often became arms and hands. From then on, offerings were to be presented only to this one, highest god. It is certain that Akhenaton made many enemies with his fanatic stand, and he was so preoccupied with religious reform that he neglected events in foreign politics. Since the pharaoh had opponents vigorously persecuted, he was also accused of founding an ancient police state.

In addition to the religious field, art was also subjected to a reorientation. Instead of the usual idealized kinds of representations that originated with the Egyptian tradition, Akhenaton demanded realistic and individual works of art. Sculptures of the king and his wife, Nefertiti, can therefore be viewed as the first realistic portraits in Egyptian history. During his time in office, there were also the first three-dimensional representations and expressions of movements and emotions. The end of Akhenaton's reign is lost in the darkness of history, and his burial place is still unknown today. After his reign there followed the rule of his son, Tutankhamen, who reversed his father's reforms to a great extent.

Symbol of androgyny and purposefulness

HATSHEPSUT

Queen Hatshepsut lived during her reign mainly in the masculine aspect of her personality. After the short reign of her husband, Thutmosis II, she pushed aside the minor Thutmosis III and had herself appointed as regent. From then on, she appeared as a man in male clothing and had herself addressed as such. Her rebellious reform-minded thinking rapidly brought her much enmity, but also astonishment. Her concepts about government must be viewed even today as very modern. Her character was described as exceptionally decisive, power-hungry, and obstinate when it came to implementing reforms. Her logical intellect and religious strictness allowed no femininity or shades of emotion to be recognized in her being. Nevertheless, this charismatic queen was able to gather devoted disciples around herself.

After the death of Hatshepsut, which was probably violent, Thutmosis III, who was the child of a concubine of her father, assumed power. To legitimize his position, he struck down the statues of the queen and had most of her representations chopped out of the monuments. In the official lists of the dynasties, the name Hatshepsut was no longer mentioned, since she was considered to be an illegal ruler.

Prototype of beauty and intelligence

CLEOPATRA

The picture on the opposite page shows a Roman portrait bust of the Egyptian queen. Her being was described as "outstanding in intelligence, education, and culture." She skillfully applied her "esprit" and her charm to win the most important men to her plans. Cleopatra embodied the concept of femininity, since she understood how to use her female energies to realize her visions. She loved both beauty and passions, as well as the power games of politics.

Cleopatra reigned initially because after the death of her father, Ptolemy XII, she drove her minor brother, Ptolemy XIII, from the throne. However, she was forced into exile in Syria. Only with the help of the Romans was she able to win back the Egyptian throne. She bore a son to the Roman Emperor, Julius Caesar. At almost the same time, she started a romantic relationship with the commander of his army, Mark Antony. From this union came a pair of twins, Alexander and Cleopatra, and their son Ptolemy Philadelphos. When Mark Antony lost then war he had instigated against Rome in 30 B.C., due to a mistaken strategy, he committed suicide. At the same time, the son of Cleopatra and Julius Caesar, Caesarion, was murdered with his father in Rome. Since Cleopatra would not allow the Romans to triumph by capturing her, she likewise chose suicide, next to her beloved Mark Antony.

Symbol of femininity — a queen who stayed politically in the background

NEFERTITI

Queen Nefertiti was the wife of the revolutionary king Amenhotep IV, who later entered history as Akhenaton. The couple were married in their youth. Nefertiti embodied the image of a woman who helped her husband to fame and respect by purposely staying in the background. The couple then implemented the revolutionary idea of the single, highest god, who was worshiped in the form of the abstract sun disk. The date of Nefertiti's death is unknown, since she is no longer mentioned after the 13th year of her marriage.

One striking innovation introduced by Akhenaton and Nefertiti was the individualized form of representation for Egyptian rulers in art, who were previously shown only as idealized form. The impressive bust of this queen is thus viewed as the first realistic picture of a queen.

Beauty and harmony

TUTANKHAMEN

This young king took office at the age of eight. His pedigree has not yet been clarified with certainty. Amenhotep IV, or Akhenaton, is suspected as his father, however. Until the second year of his reign, he kept his birth name, Tutankhaton. After that, he changed his name to Tutankhamen, which means "living image of Amun." During his reign, many monumental structures were erected, restoration work was accomplished, and unfinished projects were completed. For this reason, the name of Tutankhamen is associated with perfection, harmony, and beauty. His character was described with the following additional names: "Strong Bull with Full Birth," "He who Calms the Two Lands with Perfect Laws," and "He who Pacifies the Gods."

After the king died unexpectedly early, probably in consequence of an accident or an attack, he was quickly buried in a non-royal grave in the Valley of the Kinds. The historical importance of the child king, who only lived to eighteen years of age, is generally classified as slight.

PLANTS

1.

2.

3.

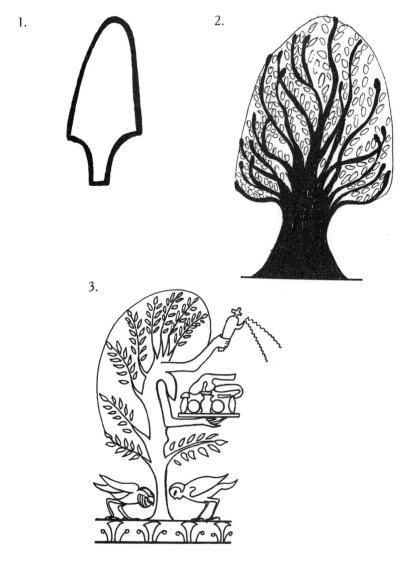

Tree and tree goddess

TREE

1. The hieroglyphic shown for "tree" contains the sound value "im."

2. This picture shows a representation of a tree in a burial chamber. Tree cults were very widespread throughout Egypt. Accordingly, many gods were also said to have come from trees. Horus came from the acacia ("in which death and life are encompassed"), Wepwawet from the tamarisk, and Re from the sycamore. Deities were also brought into connection with trees in other ways. In Memphis, the god Kheribakef ("the one under his olive tree," who merged into Ptah in the Old Kingdom. Two regions of Upper Egypt bore trees as emblems, the Sycamore Region and the Tree Region. In general, trees and humans are viewed as depending on each other. This is also shown in a story told about Bata, whose heart was located in the flowers of a cedar, for which reason he had to die when the tree was cut down.

If the tree hieroglyphic was applied directly to a coffin, this was an indication of the resurrection and meant "The coffin turns green." Pictures of trees are often found in graves, since the dead, like the living, are refreshed in their shade and enjoy their fruit.

3. This wall painting shows the soul of a deceased couple in the form of birds at a pool with lotus blossoms. The tree goddess rising above them is serving food and drink to them.

1.

2.

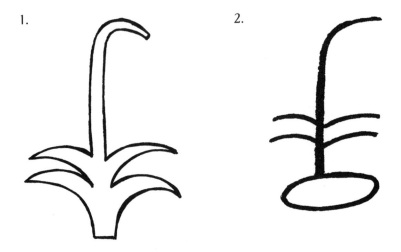

3.

Sut plants

RUSHES, SUT PLANTS

1. The hieroglyphic for the sut plant has the phonetic value "sw." In all probability, this the sut plant involves a type of rush growth from the swamps along the Nile. Since ancient times, it has been regarded as the symbol of Upper Egypt. The kings of Upper Egypt received the title "nyswt," "He who Belongs to the Sut Plant," as an additional name. By in Roman times, the real identity of this swamp plant had been lost. In any case, it denoted a region that stood in clear opposition to the dry desert.

2. This variant of the hieroglyphic denotes the south and has the sound value "rswt."

3. Here, a growth of rushes can be seen as represented in wall paintings.

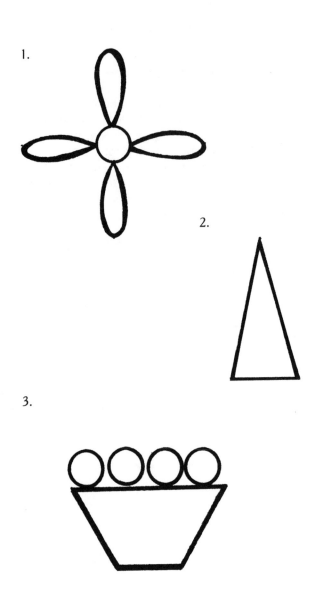

1.

2.

3.

Flowers, thorn, and plant offering

FLOWERS

1. The hieroglyphic for "flower" has the sound value "wn."

Flowers were generally presented to the gods as offerings. These flower bouquets were then often placed in containers that had the shape of the loop of life. It was believed that the gods were present in them and their aroma was equated with the fragrance of the gods. The word for "life" in the Egyptian language had the same sound as the word for flower. Pictures of flower bouquets in grave sites indicate that the deceased has gone into eternal spring. Flowers are symbols of the unfolding of life. The lotus was the first flower that came out of the original waters. Many deities were represented by flowers.

2. This ideogram stands for "srt," which means "thorn" and stands for the word "spd," which means "tip" or "sharp" and appears in connection with such words.

3. The basket with fruit is the sign for "plant offering."

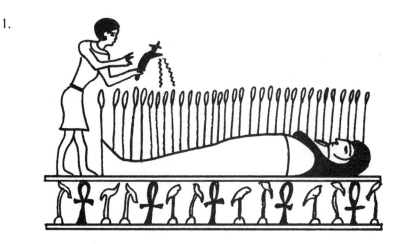

1.

2.

3.

4.

Grain mummy and grain hieroglyphics

GRAIN

1. The so-called grain mummy shows Osiris in his capacity as god of vegetation. The grain coming out of his dead body as young sprouts is a symbol of his resurrection. His bed consists of five signs of life (ankh) and ten uas scepters. As a magical aid for living after death and as a symbol of the invincibility of the dead, it was often formed from earth in the likeness of the dead person, into which grain seeds were embedded, so that fresh greens would sprout from it.

2. Barley seeds are representative of all kinds of grains, since this is the oldest known grain. They form the hieroglyphic "it" and could be arranged either side by side or one above another. The number three stands for an uncountable quantity. Grain, from which bread and beer were prepared, was generally a symbol of life-maintaining forces.

3. The "emmer" ear, which is largely unknown in our countries, was often used in Egypt for baking bread, which constituted the basis of nutrition. The emmer was also used for medical purposes, including predicting a birth.

4. The sign shown, which has the sound value "khw," shows a stylized grain sheaf and stands for the concept "heap" or "amount."

1.

2.

3.

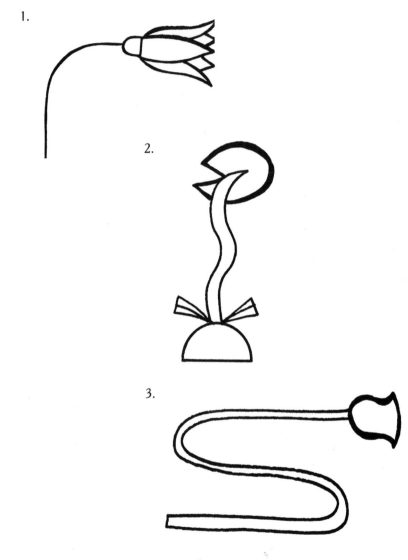

Lotus

LOTUS

1. The ideogram for lotus has the phonetic value "ssn." The lotus is a living symbol for beauty and grace. Water lilies are therefore found on almost all wall paintings, whether as lotus bouquets on columns or as graphic borders. In Egypt, there is both the white lotus and the blue lotus, which was valued more highly because of its fine, sweet fragrance. Since the plants had the characteristic of drawing their flowers deep back into the water at night and letting them appear again at daybreak, they were associated with the sun breaking forth from the night. In the Egyptian Book of the Dead, the sun god Re is "the youth who came forth from the lotus." This plant represents a connection between the divine light and the chaotic darkness. For this reason, it is a sign of hope and rebirth. The flowers of the sacred blue lotus can be seen in many graves to delight the deceased with their fragrance. This plant is assigned to the god Nefertem.

2. This sign shows a lotus stem with root tubers and leaf. The sound value is "hz." It is used often to write the number 10,000. Since the deceased hoped to enjoy ten thousand good things, this sign is often found in grave inscriptions.

3. Here, the hieroglyphic for "offering" can be seen. It shows a lotus blossom with a long stem. The sound value is "wdn." Women who presented offerings held lotus blossoms with extra long stems in their hands. The long stalks were considered to be a characteristic of beauty in flowers. Since the Egyptians liked to play with writing, the hieroglyphic for the lotus blossom was often replaced with the head of a goose.

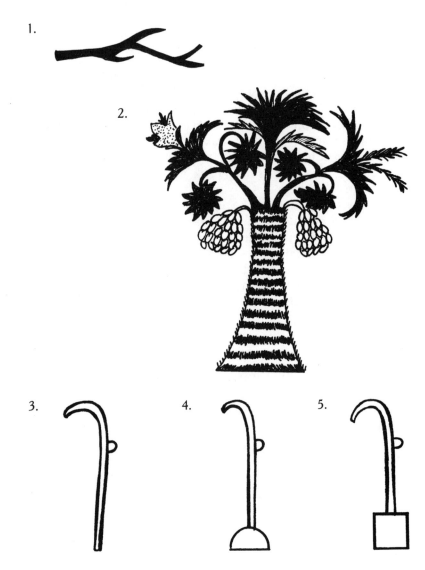

Palms and branches

PALMS AND BRANCHES

1. This early form, which was common starting with the New Kingdom, shows a branch with leaves and relates to all wooden objects. It forms the syllable "ht," which is identical with the word "wood" and also with the old expression for "tree." Plant parts and useful objects could be denoted by this ideogram.

2. The date palm, with its radiating crown, was considered to be associated with the sun and as the sacred tree of Re. It is therefore represented most often in the form of palm columns during the two periods when sun worship flourished. The goddess Hathor was sometimes called the "lady of the date palm." Sycamores and date palms enjoyed special honor in the Nile Valley as trees of life, since they only grew where sufficient life-giving water was present. The doum palm, whose stem is divided into two or three parts, was a symbol of fertility. Its representation is therefore found often in grain bins. This kind of palm was associated with both Thoth, the god in baboon form, and with the fertility god Min.

3. This ideogram shows a palm rib, and has the sound values "tr" and "rnp." Originally the branch was represented with several forks; later it was limited to one.

4. This variant of a palm rib symbolized the seasons and stands for fertility, which depended on the annual flooding of the Nile land.

5. In this form ("rnpi"), the palm-rib hieroglyphic means "to be young."

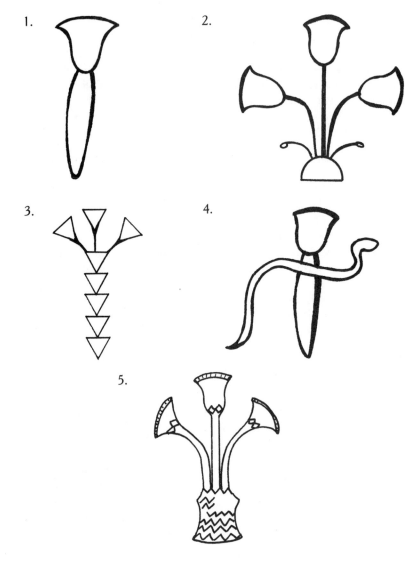

1.

2.

3.

4.

5.

Papyrus

PAPYRUS

1. Here, the hieroglyphic for papyrus stem can be seen, which has the sound value "wzd" or "wd."

The papyrus was used in old Egypt for, among other things, making light boots and for the production of sandals, mats, and clothing. It received special importance in the production of paper and scrolls. The papyrus, which grows 5 to 6 meters high, is a symbol of vitality and life force. The color green is represented with the same hieroglyphic and stands for happiness. Goddesses carry papyrus stems, which are generally associated with the symbolic power of the moon, as a scepter. In contrast to the papyrus, the sun gods arose from the lotus.

Temple frescos show papyrus columns as signs of the world arising from the original waters. They are a symbol of new creation, which manifests itself daily.

2. This ideogram shows a papyrus bundle as presented to the dead or the gods as an offering. It is a symbol of joy and victory.

3. The written sign and also the coat of arms of Lower Egypt consisted of several papyrus stems growing out a piece of land.

4. When the sign for papyrus is combined with the symbol of the cobra, the hieroglyphic for "green," "fresh," "to prosper" is formed.

5. The written sign for papyrus bundle (sound value "tz" or "mhw") was often decorated artistically. It is the symbol of the Nile Delta. Thus the wavy lines indicted the water from which the plants grow. This involves mainly the older forms of representation of the written sign of Figure 3, in which the papyrus is shown with closed buds.

1.

2.

3.

4.

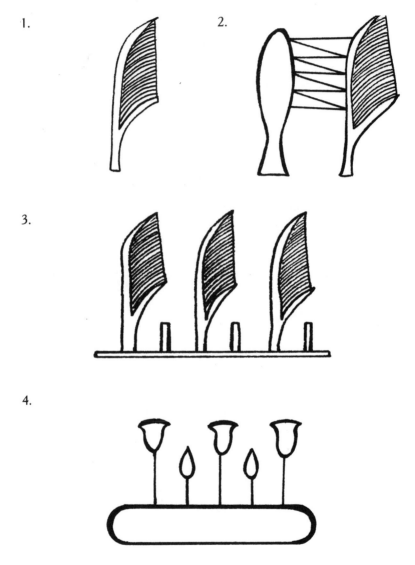

Reeds

REEDS

1. Here, the hieroglyphic for the blooming reed can be seen. As a letter, it corresponds to the sound "i."

2. With this hieroglyphic, a bundle of offerings is described. On the right stands the sign for "i," on the left the sign for "hm;" between them are bundled cone-shaped sweets.

3. The three reed blossoms stand for "land" and have the sound value "sht." The land denoted in this way relates to the cultivated, fruitful fields that arose from the water of the regions flooded by the Nile. Every year, the Nile overflowed its banks and left behind flood lands full of nutrition. The land that arose from the water was then covered with brilliant green reeds and grass.

4. This ideogram symbolizes the flooded land. Various plants are springing up from the hieroglyphic for island, the oval. Before the construction of the Aswan Dam, countless such small islands of plants and tufts arose from the Nile at high water.

1.

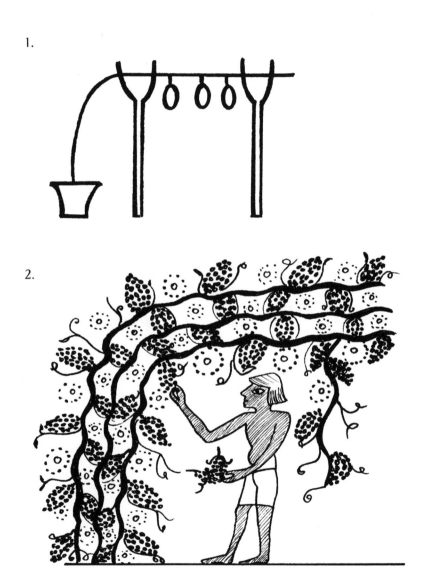

2.

Wine

WINE

1. This hieroglyphic shows a grape branch and denotes either the vineyard ("izrrt") or wine "irp"). Grapes were cultivated in Egypt in the Old Period, and their branches adorned the gardens. In religious texts grapes were called "pupils of the Horus eye" and wine "tears." The cosmic grapevine was viewed as the tree of life. Accordingly, the myth tells that Isis became pregnant after eating grapes and gave birth to her son, Horus. The god of the wine-press, Shesmu, offers wine to the dead as a life-maintaining drink. Since the Egyptians were great wine lovers, amphora with stored wine were extremely carefully provided with labels containing precise information about the source, year, and quality.

2. This segment of a wall painting, from the grave of Nakthamum, shows a grape harvest.

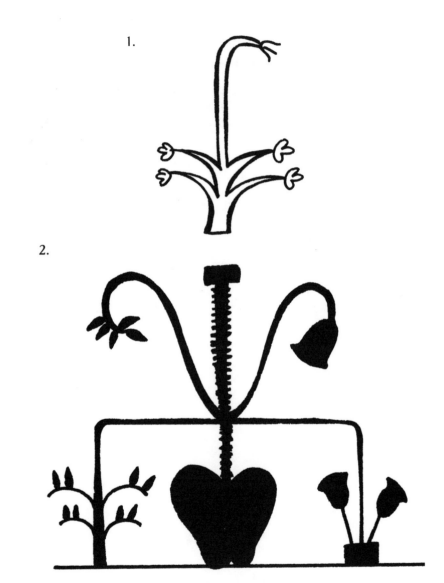

Reeds and papyrus as heraldic plants

HERALDIC PLANTS

1. The heraldic plant of Upper Egypt resembles the sut plant in its shape. The sound value is "sm." The botanical classification of this plant is still disputed today. It has been associated with either a lily or a reed.

2. In the coat of arms of the unified Upper and Lower Egypt, the two plants, reeds and papyrus, that are characteristic plants in both regions can be seen. The union of the two lands of Horus and set are represented in this way. This so-called "smz-tzwy" motif is found on the thrones of most statues of rulers erected after the unification of the two kingdoms. In addition to the gods Horus and Set, the land goddesses Buto and Nekhbet are often shown as well.

The written sign, which shows a lung with an air tube, denotes union and perfection. It is surrounded by the two heraldic plants.

ANIMALS

Antelope

ANTELOPE

In Lower Egypt, the antelope suffered a fate similar to that of all desert animals. It was despised and hunted as the embodiment of Set. Its wild temperament and the weapon-like horns of some species reinforced the folk belief that personifications of destructive powers could be seen in these animals.

In the regions of Upper Egypt near the desert, in contrast, these animals were brought into connection with the life-giving water, which can probably be attributed to a South Arabian influence. There, the rain god Attar was worshiped, whose symbolic animal was the antelope. In Elephantine, the goddess Satis, was worshiped as the giver of water, in antelope form. Also, the old sign of the sixteenth region of Upper Egypt showed a white antelope, above which a representation of a victorious Horus was added, but only in later times.

1.

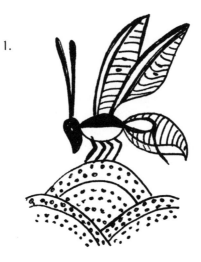

2.

Bees

BEES

1. A reproduction of a segment of a wall painting shows a bee on a honeycomb. In the extensive region of the Nile Delta, bee culture has been demonstrated since the third millennium before Christ. According to one papyrus, the beekeeper called the bees with a reed flute when he wanted them to swarm. A myth tells that once upon a time the tears wept by the sun god Re changed into bees. Therefore, representations of bees can also be found in the temples of this god. Honey was used both as a food and also in medicine as in the production of ointments. The royal names of the early dynasties of Lower Egypt preferred the additional name "Bee Prince." In later times, the pharaohs received the title "n(y)-swt-bit," "he who belongs to the reeds and the bees." The reed was considered to be the symbol of Upper Egypt. In general, bees were associated with the divine ancestral king. Accordingly, the main temple of the war goddess Neith in Sais was also called the "palace of the bee."

2. The hieroglyphic for bee is found either in this pictorial or in a reduced form. The written sign "bit" was the first written symbol for ancient Egypt.

Donkeys

DONKEY

The donkey was generally seen as the companion animal of the destructive god Set. According to the myth, 77 donkeys went against the sun to prevent it from rising in the early morning.

The general tendency against this animal, which nevertheless performed valuable services as a working animal, is probably due to its association with the Asiatic nomads who had introduced it into the land. Because of its sexual potency, the donkey was also associated with the negative aspects of dissipation. For this reason, the hieroglyphic for "phallus" was often preferred to represent the donkey in picture writing. In addition, this animal also had the task of carrying grain away, which was viewed as an embodiment of Osiris. Thus, on the occasion of the Osiris festival in the New Kingdom, a donkey was ritually stabbed with lances in order to break the destructive power of Set. Based on this custom, the hieroglyphic for "donkey" was usually written with a knife between the shoulder blades. According to the myth, donkey-headed demons also guarded the gates to the underworld.

Owl

OWL

The owl was the only living being depicted with its face turned to face the front. Most likely this was done in order to emphasize its ability to turn its head extremely far.

Many circumstances indicate that the owl was considered to be an unlucky bird, based on its eerie look and silent nightly flight. Also its unsettling call, which could be heard at night, brought it near to the dark powers of the underworld. Probably for this reason, all mummies of these birds that have been found have the head cut off. Also the hieroglyphic for the expression "to cut the head off a bird" consists of a picture of an owl and the alphabetic letter "k."

Nile perch

FISH

In ancient Egypt, fish were generally viewed as unclean animals, and holy persons, such as kings and priests, were forbidden to eat their meat. Their living space, the dark and slimy waters or the feared sea, allowed it to be appear in association with Set. In addition, a myth was told that a Nile carp, together with Phragos and Mormyrus, had eaten the penis of Osiris, who had been cut into pieces. Accordingly, on the occasion of certain festival days, the gods were offered fish, which were then crushed or burned in order to demonstrate victory over the dark powers. An exception, however, was the Nile perch, a fish that hatches its young in its mouth and then later provides them protection in this way. The swallowing and subsequent rebirth of the children corresponded to the sun cycle and made the Nile perch a powerful symbol of rebirth after death.

In Mendes, the goddess Hatmehit was also worshiped, who was viewed as the "first of the fishes" and wore the sign of a dolphin on her head.

Phoenix bird, heron

SYMBOLIC ANIMAL OF RENEWAL: PHOENIX BIRD, HERON

The phoenix was the sacred bird of Heliopolis. Its Egyptian name, Boinu, derived from the words for "to shine" and "to rise."

This bird involves a heron, which visited the Nile Valley in large numbers at the times of the floods. Its cyclic return, which was associated with the life-giving power of the water, made it into a symbol of eternal renewal.

Already in ancient times, the heron became the sun bird, since, like the sun, it habitually rose from the waters to the sky in the early morning to greet the dawn. The myth of self-immolation and resurrection likewise derives from this image.

Beginning in ancient Egypt, concepts about the time intervals between its returns differed widely from one another. There are reports of a time of fifty years and also a period of 1,461 years. The latter information relates to the Sothis period, which coincided with the setting of the star Sirius. Each new cycle of Sirius was viewed as a complete reordering of the cosmos and the start of a new era.

The connection with the sun made the phoenix the ba of Re, and its relationship to the kingdom of the dead and its resurrection from its own ashes allowed it to become a manifestation of Osiris.

Frog

FROG

The hieroglyphic of the frog was viewed as the symbol of a human that had not yet been formed. Accordingly, it was also the frog-headed goddess Heket who was responsible for the formation of the fetus in the mother's womb. She also guarded birth as a midwife.

The origin of life was associated with the slimy depths of the water, in which it just teems before life. Therefore, in the story of the origin of the world in Heliopolis Magna, the original deity is described as a snake- or frog-headed creature. In the New Kingdom, the frog became the symbol of the "repetition of life."

Goose and Eggs

GOOSE

Because of its special thoughtfulness and parental love, the goose was given special recognition in Egypt. Accordingly, this hieroglyphic often stood for the word "son," and it is therefore found in many texts and inscriptions, especially in genealogies, where names of family members are listed. The Egyptians ascribed a special relationship between animals and the original god, Amun, who sometimes is himself represented as a goose. Thus the symbolism of the egg made the goose a partial aspect of the original legend. According to tradition, the first god arose from a wonderful egg that came forth from the original waters.

As the seat of burgeoning life, eggs were accompanied by many taboos. Accordingly, priests were forbidden to eat them, and even in pictures they were never depicted as food, although the people surely ate the eggs of various kinds of birds.

Like all round things, the egg as a closed symbol also stood for eternal life and resurrection. In the necropolises of the sacred birds, therefore, next to the mummies of animals, their eggs can also be found, likewise bound with bandages. The innermost coffin, which enclosed the mummy, was called "egg," since it was the shell of the life that would arise anew in the otherworld. As a hieroglyphic, it also represented "body cloth" in addition to "sarcophagus," and it could also stand for childhood.

Egg-shaped amulets were generally popular as carriers of the original divine force and were also buried with the dead.

Gazelle and desert rabbit

GAZELLE

In the understanding of the ancient Egyptians, the gazelle played a double role. On the one hand, it is found in peaceful scenes as a domesticated house animal, and on the other hand it was considered in its wild form as a form of the god Set.

To the inhabitants of Lower Egypt, which was rich in vegetation, the wild gazelle that lived in the hostile desert was an enemy. Since it lived in the life-threatening realm of the god Set, it was also counted as one of his followers. Gazelles were often sacrificed during religious ceremonies in order to protect against evil forces.

In the drier parts of Upper Egypt, in contrast, these animals were assigned a divine status because of their speed and grace. The goddess Anuket was worshiped in the city of Komir in the form of a gazelle and had the additional names "princess of the gods" and "lady of the sky."

RABBIT

The rabbit, because of its special abilities, its rapid running, and its exceptional sense perception, was assigned divine powers. Its written sign shows the extremely enlarged ears as an indication of the animal's alertness. This hieroglyphic stands for the verb "to run."

Rabbit figures were also popular as amulets, especially in the later period. In Upper Egypt, the animals were viewed as followers of the goddess Unut, who stood at the head of the 15th Region. Unut had human form and carried a standard with a recumbent rabbit on her head.

Ichneumon and lapwing

ICHNEUMON

The ichneumon is a subtype of the mongoose, which is related to the civet. Its pronounced enmity to snakes made the related meerkat a symbolic animal of Horus. According to a myth, this god changed itself into the ichneumon in order to fight the Apophis snake of the underworld.

These animals were generally worshiped as benevolent spirits of the underworld, and sculptures of them were decorated with sun symbols, later also with the uraeus snake.

LAPWING

This picture of the rekhit bird, which was also used as a hieroglyphic, is easily recognizable as a lapwing. This migratory bird, which comes from Europe, appeared in large numbers as a winter guest in the Nile Delta. Its hieroglyphic corresponded to the phonetic value "rhyt" (hence rekhit), the word for foreigners who were, to certain degree, integrated into the Egyptian kingdom. Therefore, they were also regarded as subjects of the pharaoh. This bird was considered to be a symbol of foreigners who were tolerated in the land, but were often viwed with mistrust or even hostility.

1.

2.

Crocodile

CROCODILE

1. The powerful, destructive powers of the crocodile were generally feared. In ancient Egypt, the Nile crocodile, which was associated with the god Set, was still widespread and caused considerable damage. Its hieroglyphic, corresponding to its characteristics, also stood for "to be greedy" or "to be voracious." In general, this animal was treated with respect, as it was said that only the power of love could conquer the raw power of the crocodile.

2. In the Upper Egyptian Fayum and in Kom Ombo, the crocodile god Sebek was worshiped. He was represented either as a crocodile on the sacred shrine or as a human with a crocodile head. According to folk belief, the Nile originated from the sweat of this god. The massive appearance of these animals during the annual floods brought them into association with rich harvests. Sebek therefore received his significance as a fertility god. In later times, this god was included in the cult of Re and received its attributes, such as the hawk head and sun disk, as Sebek-Re.

Hathor as goddess of the dead in cow form

COW

Cows were the sacred animals of the goddess Hathor. Since the king himself was often depicted as a bull, the cow assumed symbolically the position of his mother. In the myth told about the divine birth of the ruler, the sacred Hesath cow suckled the youth. The mystification of this animal was based on the worship of the sky cow, who joined the sky with the underworld and thereby guaranteed life after death. Accordingly, the catafalques on which the biers rested during ceremonies for the dead had the shape of a cow. The Hesath cow received special respect as the mother of the Apis bull and the god Anubis.

This sculpture shows the goddess Hathor in the form of a cow as goddess of the dead.

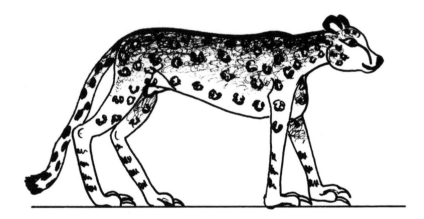

Leopard

LEOPARD

The leopard or panther was considered to be the embodiment of the goddess Maftet, who was authorized to lead the living and the dead to their just punishments. However, as a being of justice, its task also included helping the dead. For this reason, the skin of this wild cat was painted on many coffins, and the mouth-opening priests dressed themselves in panther skins. The custom of wrapping the dead in leopard skins probably derived from an older tradition that was observed by many tribes in Africa.

In the form of an amulet, the panther head was to confer the power to overcome death.

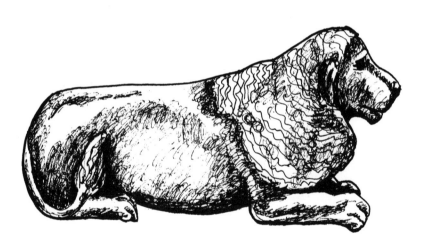

Lion

LION

The lion, which was represented as either lying casually or striding proudly, was considered to be a manifestation of the sun god. Since this animal was associated with the sun cycle, and thereby also embodied death and rebirth, biers were often given its shape.

In a recumbent pose, it radiated the majestic rest of a ruler; in this form, the image of the sphinx was also connected with it. In contrast, the striding attitude referred to its wildness and its courage. The king himself was glad to be equated with the lion as a strong, powerful warrior, and he was therefore often depicted hunting or in battle, accompanied by lionesses. Lion hunting was a exclusive privilege of the pharaohs.

Through its frightening appearance, the lion was also viewed as the watcher of the king's throne, which was provided with the legs and tail of a lion for this purpose. As a statue, it was the guardian of the temple entrance; also the entrance to the underworld was guarded by the two lion-heads of the god Aker.

The lion-shaped deities worshiped most were female and were associated with battle and the element fire. In addition to the goddesses Sekhmet and Mehit, there was in Leontopolis also the pair of lions, Ruti, which symbolized the male and female creative powers and guarded offerings to the dead.

Shrew

SHREW

In Letopolis, the shrew was considered to be a sacred animal of Horus; it embodied its dark, nightly aspect. This animal, which sees poorly and lives underground, formed an opposite to the hawk, the being of light.

Since the shrew was found mainly in its dark realm, it was associated with the re-creation of the sun during the night. The drawing on the opposite page relates to this myth. All figures and drawings show the shrew in a vertical position, covered with symbols of the sun god. Mummies of this animal have also been found.

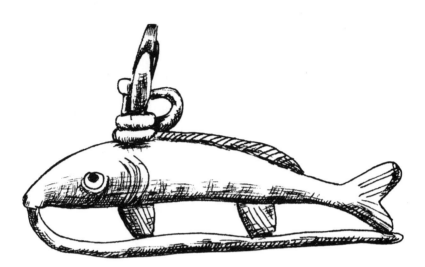

Nile pike and hippopotamus

NILE PIKE

The worship of the small Nile pike Oxyrhynchos was limited to the region of the Middle Egyptian city of the same name. Its name means "pointed nose," and its hieroglyphic has the sound value "hz." As emblems, it carried the sun disk and cow horns on its head, which assigned it as a follower of the goddess Hathor. This fish was said to have came originally from the wounds of Osiris.

HIPPOPOTAMUS

In the Old Kingdom, the hippopotamus was counted as a follower of Set. Based on this view, it was also a custom to kill one of the king's white hippopotamuses during the hippopotamus festival. The ruler assumed the identity of Horus in this way, in order to destroy Set in this animal form. This animal received its ugly voice through its voracity, with which was able to cause great damage to fields.

The female animals, however, were associated with pregnant women, because of their round body shape, which contributed to their deification. In the New Kingdom, the hippopotamus goddess Taurt achieved great popularity, and biers also received a hippopotamus shape. In this way, this animal became a general fertility symbol.

1.

2.

Baboon

BABOON

1. The baboon was considered a sacred animal and was dedicated to the god Thoth.

2. Its hieroglyphic "knd," stands for "to be furious," and its denotation as an animal. Thoth was the god of the art of writing and the sciences. In his manifestation as a baboon, he served as a prototype of the lively and intelligent animal for listless students. Because of the exceptionally active love life of the apes, its excrement was also used as an aphrodisiac.

Originally, the baboon god Hez-ur was worshiped in the Middle Egyptian city Hermopolis, which later merged with the ibis-headed god Thoth. From then on, it was considered to be an incarnation of Thoth, the "lord of the moon." One story tells how this god, in the form of the baboon Tefnut, reconciles the daughter of Re with her father after a dispute. The goddess had withdrawn as a sun cat far to the south, where the clever ape tracked her down and got her, through all kinds of tricks, to return to the north for a while and reunite with her father. This myth is based on the lowering of the sun's path in winter and its return to the north in spring.

Horse

HORSE

The battle scene depicted shows king Tutankhamen in an imaginary battle against Asians. His pose in the chariot, which is being pulled by two horses, shows him as a brave warrior, "a brave one, without equal."

The horse first came to Egypt relatively late, through the Asiatic area. Its hieroglyphic means the same as "lord of the foreign lands," and was often used as a title with the additional name "the beautiful one." This animal quickly became a respected status symbol for the ruling class. Nevertheless, it was considered to be improper to appear in the saddle, on horseback. Instead, the custom was adopted from the Asiatic peoples of being pulled in light chariots.

The fiery temperament of the horse and its delicate grace are especially emphasized in the representations. In this way, the characteristic strength of the charioteer, to whom the animal subordinates its will, is also depicted.

1.

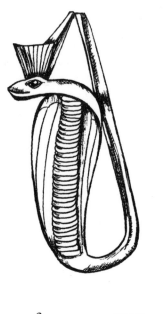

2.

Snake

SNAKE

1. Both the god Re and the pharaohs wore a threateningly erect cobra on their foreheads as protection against enemies. This symbol, which is also called the uraeus snake, was the flaming eye of the god, which destroyed enemies through the power of fire. The cobra was also considered to be a symbol of the goddess Buto, and it was associated with other goddesses as well. Buto was worshiped in the prehistoric kingdom of Buto, where she settled onto the head of the king in the form of the uraeus. Later, in the pharaonic kingdom, the fire-breathing cobra was described as the fiery sun eye of Re. This animal can be found in every royal representation, including all reliefs and sculptures. Through its close relationship wit the sun god, Re, the cobra became the heraldic animal of Lower Egypt.

In the texts fo the Egyptian Book of the Dead, the snakes' ability to become young and to be reborn each day is also mentioned, which in turn gives rise to associations with the sun disk.

2. This picture from the mysteries of the Egyptian Book of the Dead relates to the snake as a symbol of renewal, which is shows by means of human legs. The drawing is associated with the following saying, which was thought to male it possible to assume the form of a snake: "I am a snake with many years, I go through the night and am born again every day. I am a snake, the ends of the earth; I go through the night and am born again, renewed, and rejuvenated day after day."

Pig

PIG

Pigs were considered to be unclean in ancient Egypt and were assigned as followers of the god Set because of their destructive wildness and voracity. According to the Book of the Dead, Set could also transform himself into a black boar, as when he attacked Horus and injured his eye. In many reliefs and paintings, the pig therefore appears as the epitome of evil. On the occasion of the great moon festival, pigs were sacrificed to the moon deities Isis and Osiris.

The sky god Nut was described in one legend as a sow who eats her own piglets, the stars, in the morning dawn and gives birth to them again every evening (cf. p. 99). For this reason, amulets were also used that show of mother sow with her piglets as a symbol of the unconquerable source of life.

Apis bull with sun disk

BULL

Even in the oldest periods, the bull was considered to be the carrier of life force. Accordingly, the fruitful flooding of the Nile was also described as the "gift of the bull." In early times, the king was often identified directly with the bull and represented in this form in pictures. Even the rulers of the New Kingdom often bore the additional name "Strong Bull."

While the bull was originally a fertility symbol exclusively, the sacred Apis bull of Memphis was given other characteristics. From this time on, it was considered to be the earthly embodiment of the god Ptah. After his death, it became god of the dead through association with Osiris. The task of the bull also included carrying the mummy of a deceased person on its back to be buried.

This bronze figure from the late period shows the Apis bull with the sun disk on its head.

Millipede and Ram

MILLIPEDE

The Egyptian giant millipede, which grows up to twenty-five cm long, was feared because of its poisonous bite. On the other hand, this animal was valued as a pest exterminator. In order to come to an arrangement with the millipede, it was elevated to a deity. The god Sepa was worshiped in the region of Heliopolis and invoked for protection against pests.

As a hieroglyphic, as in the picture on the opposite page, it also stands for the sedan chair of the pharaoh, which was used on special festival days. The twenty bearers, who were led by a chief bearer, aroused associations with the 42 legs of the millipede. The number 42 also refers to the twenty-four provinces of Egypt and the 42 relics of the god Osiris.

RAM

Like the bull, the ram was also a symbol of fertility. It was viewed as a manifestation of the god Khnemu or else of Amun. The Amun ram can be recognized by its horns, which are turned downward.

The ram was considered to be a symbol of the cosmic foursome, since it was described as the life of Re, the life of Shu, the life of Geb, and the soul of Osiris. In this way, the image of god with four heads on one neck arose.

Hoopoe and goat

HOOPOE

The hoopoe can be seen in many pictures in company with children, whom it served as a happy playmate.

In folk belief, it was considered to be the only animal that returned the life given it by its parents by taking care of them when they became old. In its characteristic as a symbol of gratitude, it was often associated with child deities and represented together with them.

BILLY GOAT

Only in the city of Mendes was the sacred billy goat Ba-neb-Djet worshiped as the highest lord of the city. Women prayed to this god for fertility and the ability to reproduce to fulfill their wish for children. Mummies of this sacred animal have been found in Mendes.

The goat did not achieve any great religious significance throughout the land, but it remained the sacrificial animal of simple people.

INDEX

About the author and illustrator

Heike Owusu obtained a spiritual world view very early, triggered by misunderstanding in her family and social environment. When a serious illness threatened her life, she overcame it by means of autogenous training and a self-healing method she developed herself. Her interest in the knowledge of primitive peoples and their mythologies, which was already strong, was strengthened even more by her marriage to a man from Ghana. All this released her artistic potential, and thus today she communicates her knowledge in various ways and manners: in the form of cosmic pictures, illustrations, and literary work.